Hanne Sonne

Christmas Cones in Bobbin Lace

Akacia

Christmas Cones in Bobbin Lace
By Hanne Sonne

© 2005 Forlaget Akacia
Skovvænget 1
5690 Tommerup
Denmark
akacia@akacia.dk

© All rights reserved. No part of this book may be reproduced in any
form, by print, photo print, microfilm, microfiche, mechanical recording,
photocopying, translation, or by any means, known or as yet unknown,
or stored in any information retrieval system without prior written
permission being obtained from the publishers.

Printed at Økotryk I/S, Videbæk, Denmark, 2005

ISBN-10: 87-7847-095-1
ISBN-13: 9788778470959

Foreword

The cone is one of the oldest kinds of Christmas tree decoration and of course its use is particularly connected with the idea of decorating the tree with something eatable. It is probably a luxury variation of the grocer's way of wrapping candy. The cone has evolved and become finer over the years. First cones were made from paper but today they are made from all kinds of materials.

To me a bobbin lace cone symbolises real luxury. It is a spider's web with a handle – where light is reflected off the gold, silver and beads, making them sparkle.

In this book I have played with the many variations on the lace cone. I have made them big and small, coarse and fine – depending on where – and for what you want to use them. Cones don't have to be used only for nuts; they can be hung in a doorway, a large window, in a corner – everywhere you want something decorative.

It is my wish, that you will enjoy working the cones and that you will find new ways of using them – especially during Christmas time.

Use a cone as a gift – fill it with goodies and give it to someone you care about.

    Enjoy your lacemaking.

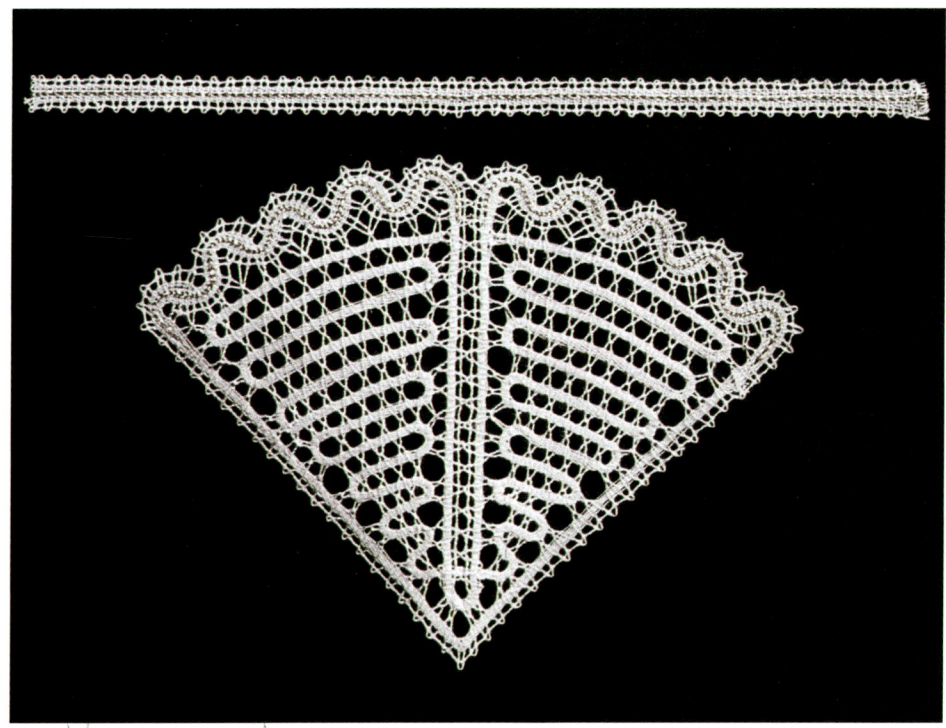

The shape of the cone and the types of lace

All the cones are the same shape – as shown on the picture – but made using different techniques.

Most of them are made in tape lace so they can be finished invisibly with a tape.

Cones No. 1, 2, 3, 8, 9, 10, 15 and 17 are all worked in the Russian tape lace technique with the traditional filling of plaits and picots and the gimp in the middle of the tape. You can hardly think of Russian tape lace without this gimp.

Cones No. 11 and 12 are worked in the Idrijan style. Idrija is a town in what is now Slovenia. Here another type of lace developed, typified by long, narrow tapes, as shown in the picture above.

Cones No. 4, 5, 6, 7 are all inspired by Czech lace art, and are worked in bands.

For the big korse cones No. 13, 14 and 16 I have played around with the techniques. This is tape lace with more free style fillings.

Before and after you work a cone

Before

Because the finished work is to be starched it is important to remember to use thick paper or pricking card, covered with film. Prick all the holes – it gives a more precise pattern in stead of making the pinholes as you work. Tension all the pairs every time you place a pin – this gives a finer, more even piece of lace. Push all the pins into the cushion while you work – this gives a better shape to your piece of lace. When there are 2 or more twists at a pin, then place half the twists before the pin, the rest after it. All the twists have a tendency to assemble either before or after the pin.

In the middle tape of the Russian tape laces, don't twist the worker before sewing the two tapes together. You work like this: In tape no. 2, remove the twist from the worker when you sew into the other tape. Replace the pin, take one bobbin behind the pin and continue working the tape, with no twists on the workers. In that way tape 2 maintains its full width. When you finish a tape don't sew in too tightly – the cone will be starched and is only a decoration. It is also very important all the eyes at the edge are clear after sewing in.

Idrija Lace was originally made using only whole stitch and whole stitch with a twist, but in modern times, half and other stitches have been added.
At the inner curve of the tape, every turn is worked by changing the workers – no pins – and the outer curve with sewings in. The pins are set between the two tapes. Normally you find a lot of twists on the worker pair between the tapes, but that's up to the lace maker depending in the weight of thread how many you want to apply. The tapes meet at the centre of the vertical or horizontal lines. The pin is set on the dot. When two tapes are joined with a sewing, remove the pin from the first tape and pull the worker neatly into place.

After
Starch

It is important that the cone is starched firmly. Use the transparent starch from Belgium. Apply it directly from the bottle, making sure it is applied evenly.
To avoid a film covering the lace lift it a little way from the pattern (still hanging on the pins), then dry with a hairdryer.
Restarch and dry it again. If you can see any remains of starch, remove it by brushing with a small stiff brush.
A good alternative is the starch from Moravia – but it has to be diluted with water.

Stitching

All the cones must appear 3-dimensional – not flat. Shape the cone over your hand or a styropor cone. Start stitching it together from the bottom. When finished, starch the join.

Storage

Make cardboard cones to place inside the lace cones to keep their shapes when storing them. That ought to keep them nice for next Christmas.

Symbols

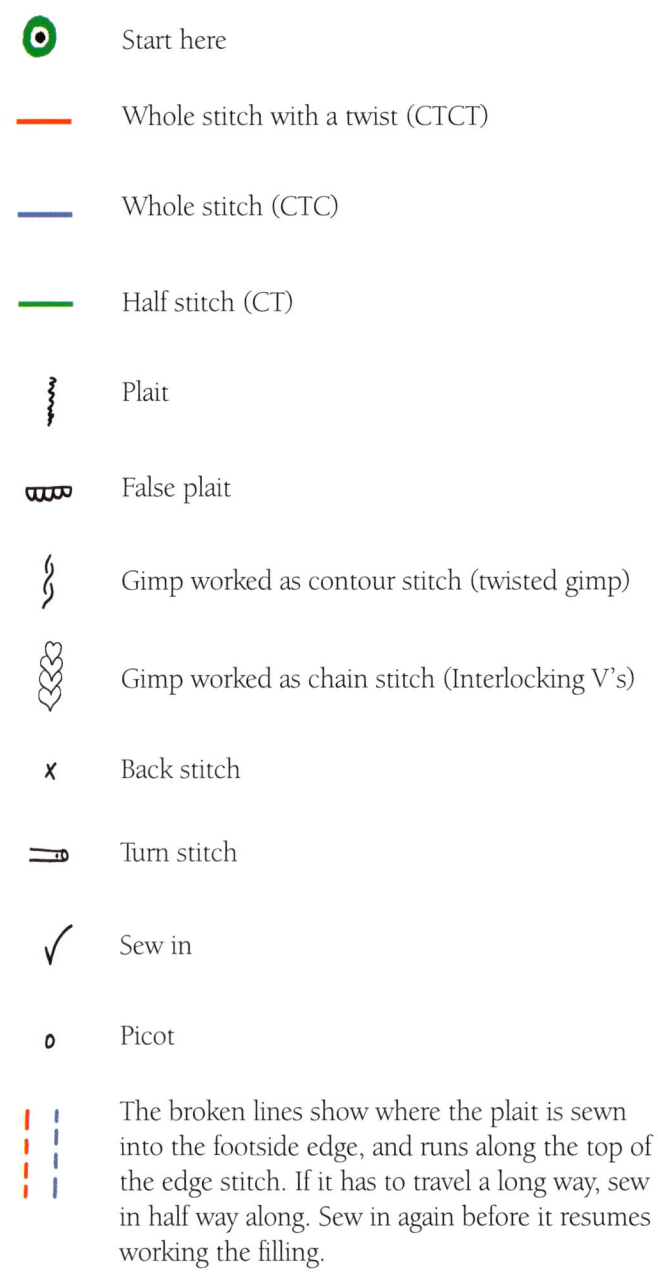

●   Start here

▬   Whole stitch with a twist (CTCT)

▬   Whole stitch (CTC)

▬   Half stitch (CT)

    Plait

    False plait

    Gimp worked as contour stitch (twisted gimp)

    Gimp worked as chain stitch (Interlocking V's)

x   Back stitch

    Turn stitch

✓   Sew in

o   Picot

The broken lines show where the plait is sewn into the footside edge, and runs along the top of the edge stitch. If it has to travel a long way, sew in half way along. Sew in again before it resumes working the filling.

To begin in whole stitch

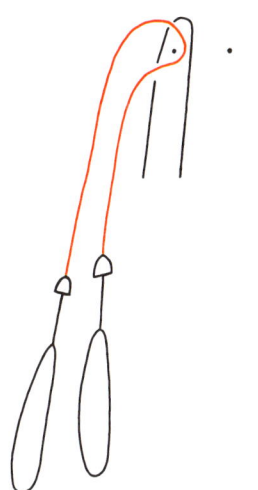

1. Set the first pin, hang on one pair and the worker pair.

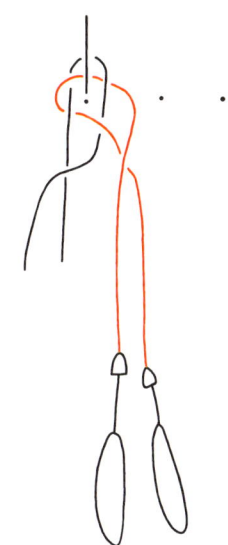

2. If working a twisted edge, whole stitch and twist.

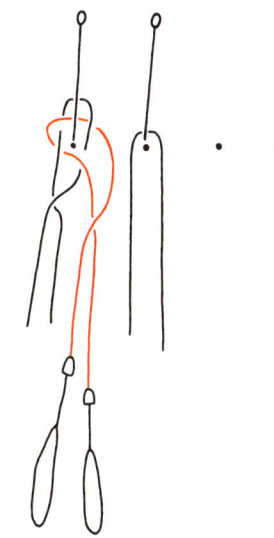

3. A new pair is added. Whole stitch. Pin up and replace the pin in the same hole, with the threads of the worker pair on either side of the pin.

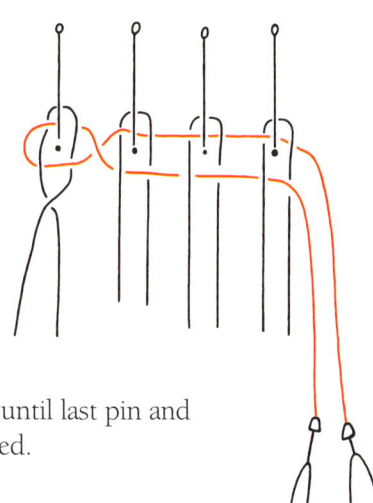

4. Repeat until last pin and pair is added.

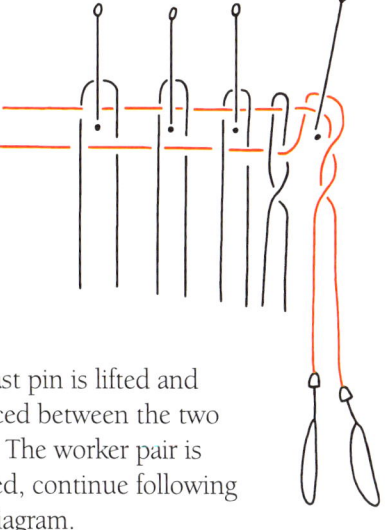

5. Last pin is lifted and replaced between the two pairs. The worker pair is twisted, continue following the diagram.

7

Sewing in at the edge

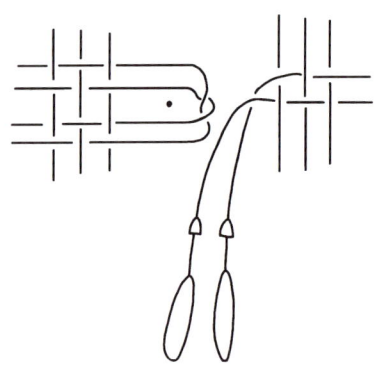

1. The pair is ready on the right hand side.

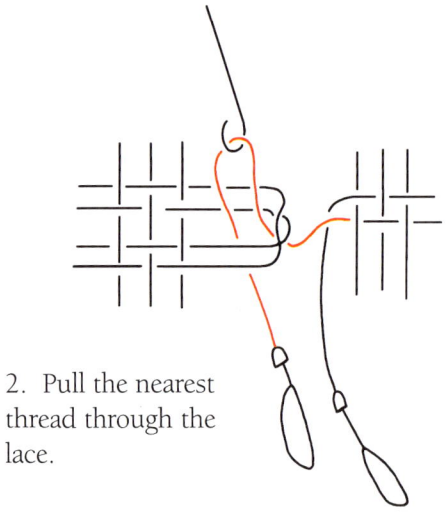

2. Pull the nearest thread through the lace.

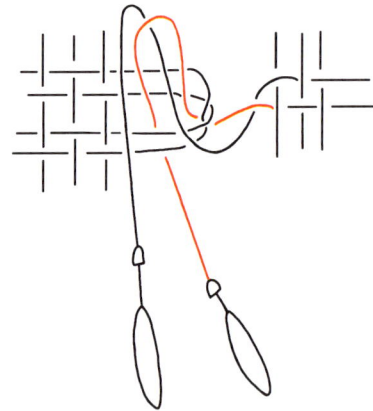

3. The right bobbin is put through the loop and is placed on the left.

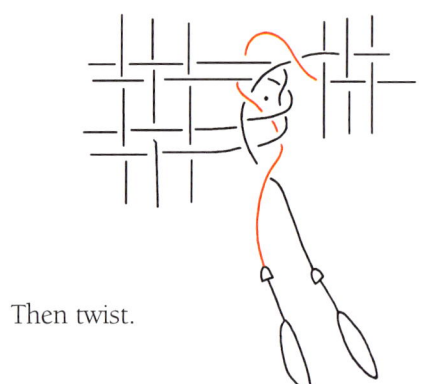

4. Then twist.

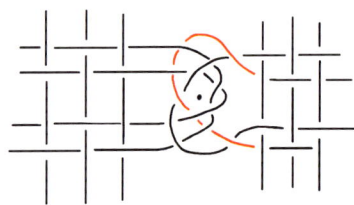

5. Leave the pin in if possible.

> If you take a pair from the left, be sure to add an extra twist before sewing in – one twist disappears when the left bobbin is put through the loop.

Sewing in - making a raised sewing

When sewing in you create a raised effect – a "hill" on the right side of the lace. To obtain this effect you have to sew in at a straight edge. You sew into the bar above or below the pins, as best suits the line of the work.

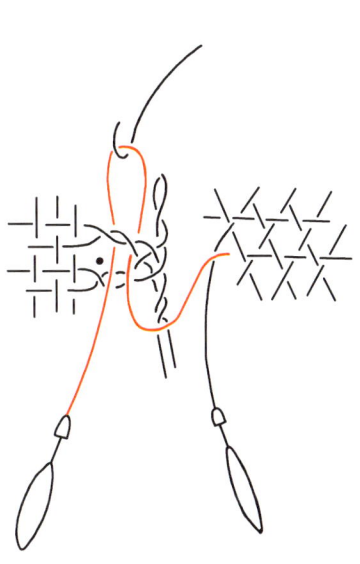

1. The nearest bobbin is pulled over the edge and under the thread above the pin.

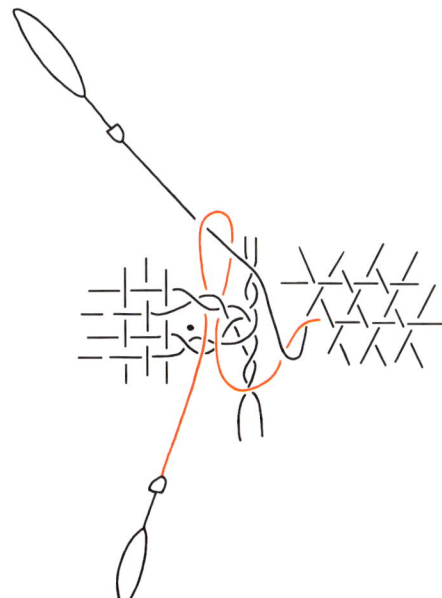

2. The second bobbin is put through the loop. Pull the pair tight and continue the lace.

Turn stitch

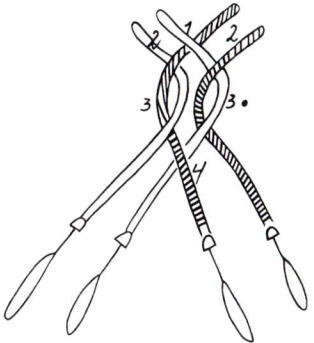

1: cross
2: twist
3: twist
4: cross

The pin is placed inside both pairs.
Remember to remove the pin after the turn stitch and carefully pull the inner pair to maintain a straight edge.

Back stitch

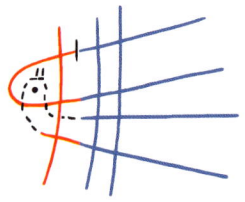

Back stitch = when you use a pin twice
1st time: Work as usual – whole stitch and a twist before and after the pin.
2nd time: Instead of working the edge stitch, add 2 twists to the workers. Take them behind the pin (on top of the edge pair), work a whole stitch and twist and continue in whole stitch.

Gimp

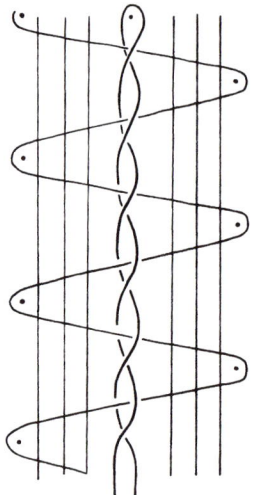

1. Gimp – twisted (contour thread).

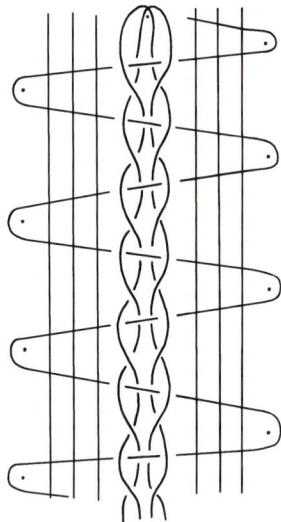

2. Gimp – interlocking V's (chain stitch).

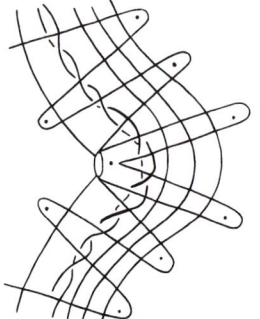

3. Gimp – in a curve. If the space is too narrow, only twist every other time.

10

Windmill crossing

When two plaits cross each other work a whole stitch with one pair acting as a bobbin.

Plait

Start a plait with a whole stitch and then alternately twists and crosses.

False Plait

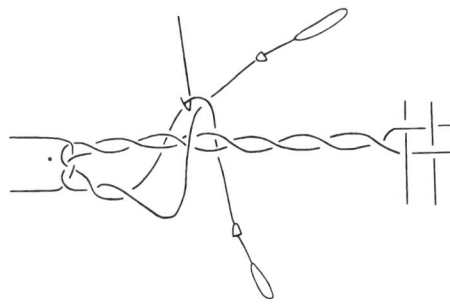
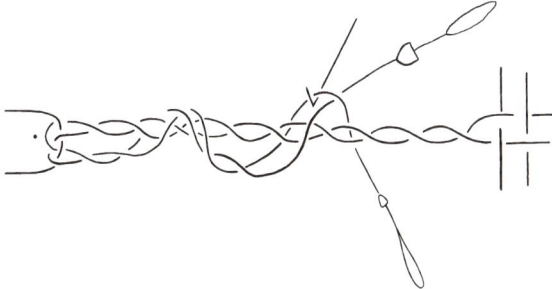

1. When you work a false plait you only work with one pair.
This pair is twisted an appropriate number of times and is sewn in on the opposite side. On the way back, twist twice and sew in around the twisted "bar".

2. Make 2 more twists and sew in again. Sew in as many times as necessary for the distance between the two tapes. The last 2 twists are situated very closely to the tape where the pair originally came from.

Two plaits crossing at a 90 degree angle

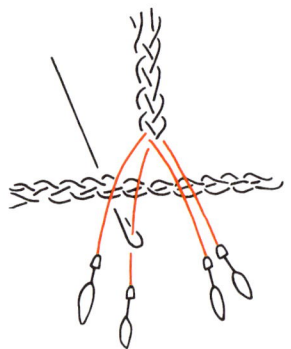

1. When 2 plaits cross at a 90 degree angle, use 2 threads – one from each pair. From left you pull the loop out under the plait.

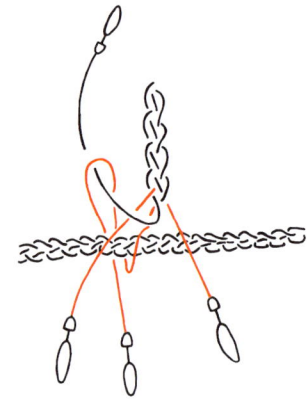

2. The left bobbin from the right pair is put through the loop. Pull tight and start the plait again with a whole stitch.

Sewing in plaits

A simple way of joining two plaits. A plait is sewn in to an existing plait and in doing so changes direction.

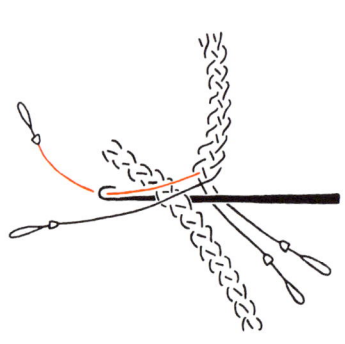

1. Sew in with the closest pair. From right pull out a loop from under the plait.

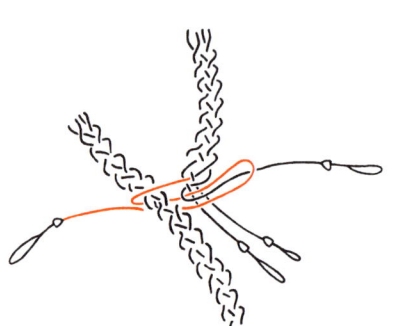

2. Put the second bobbin through the loop.

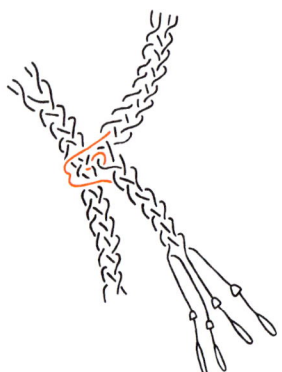

3. Pull the pair tight and start the plait again with a whole stitch.

Sewing in crossing plaits or tallies

Method 1

Join all the plaits in one sewing - under the plait, not into it. This is done the last time you pass the centre. This is a good method – giving a firm centre.

> It is ok to use support pins to help keep the plait in shape – but remember to remove them before you starch the lace.

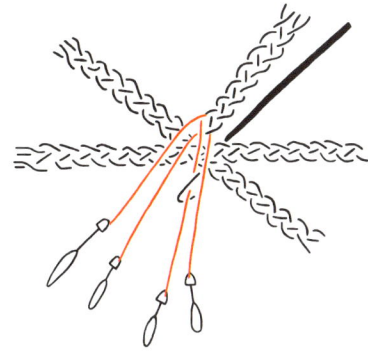

1. First sew in the right pair. Pull out a loop from under the plait.

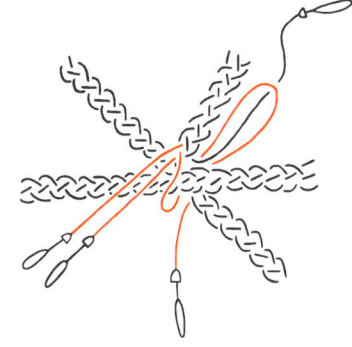

2. Put the second bobbin through the loop and pull.

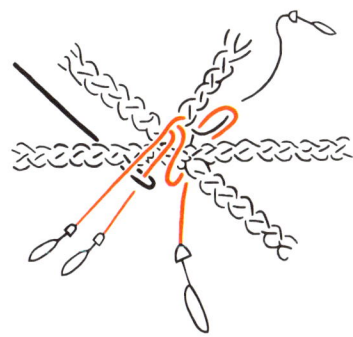

3. Then sew in the left pair. Pull out a loop from under the plait.

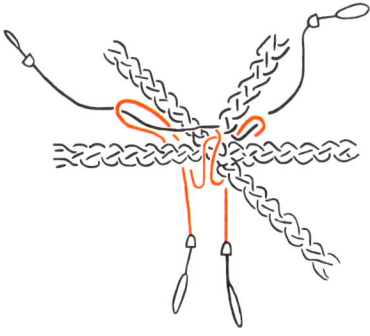

4. Put the second bobbin through the loop and pull. Start the plait with a whole stitch.

13

Sewing in crossing plaits or tallies

Method 2

Use this method if you have to make a sharp turn round a pin. It gives a good solid sewing when needed.

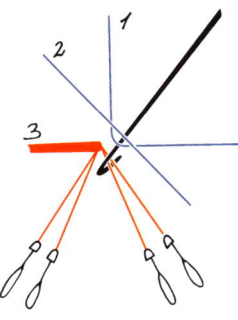

1. Plait 3 is sewn into plaits 1 and 2. Sew in with pairs.

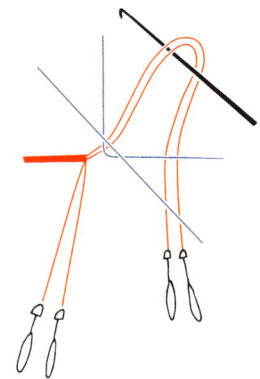

2. Pull a loop out under the plait.

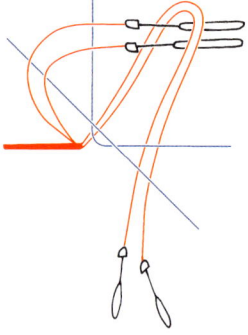

3. Put the other pair through the loop.

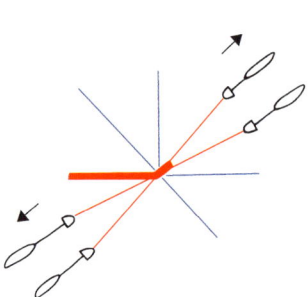

4. Pull the pairs as show on the diagram.

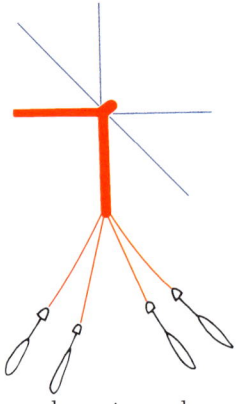

5. Replace the pairs and start again with a whole stitch.

2 thread picots with 6 twists

In the Russian Tape lace you often find picots used to decorate plaits. You find picots on both the right hand side and the left hand side. Shown here is a twisted picot with 6 twists – but the number of twists depends on the thickness of the thread.

Right hand picot

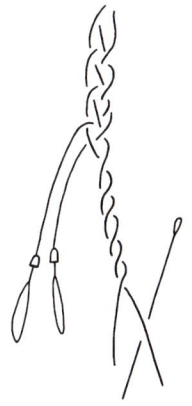

1. Twist the right pair 6 times.

2. Hold the pair in your left hand. Take a pin in your right hand and wrap the right hand thread around the pin.

3. Set the pin.

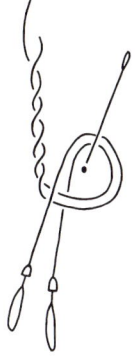

4. Carefully pull the right bobbin. The thread from the left bobbin will, because of the many twists, be pulled around the pin. Help the thread from the left bobbin around the pin and replace the bobbin.

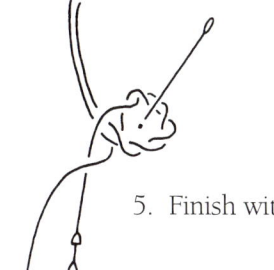

5. Finish with a twist.

Left hand picot

Follow the same procedure as for the right hand picot.

1.

2.

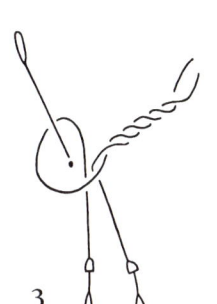

3.

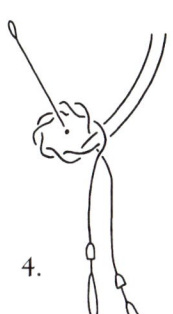

4.

Russian spider with plaits

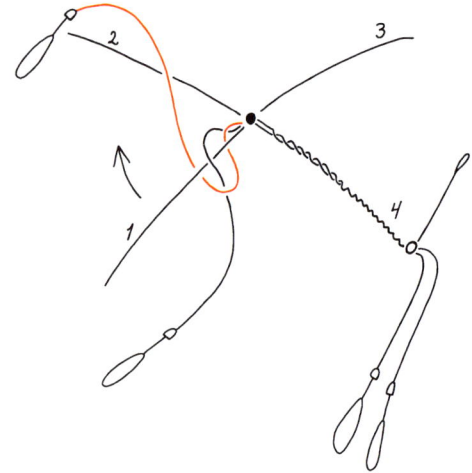
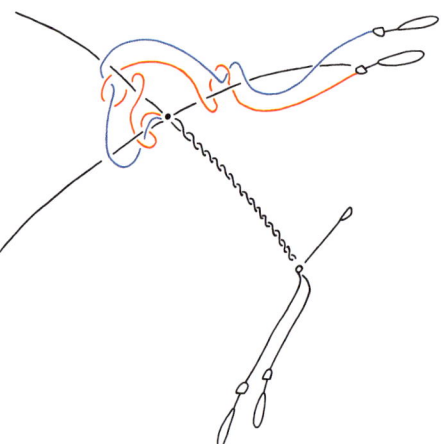

1. The numbers 1, 2 and 3 indicate the finished plaits. Work to the middle of the plaits. Use one pair to make the spider. Pull a loop from under the plait – put the other bobbin through and pull tight. The other pair is twisted and secured to a pin – perhaps outside the pricking. This is the spider's leg no. 4 (= 4).

2. Work the spider with the "spider pair". The spider actually consists of sewings in.

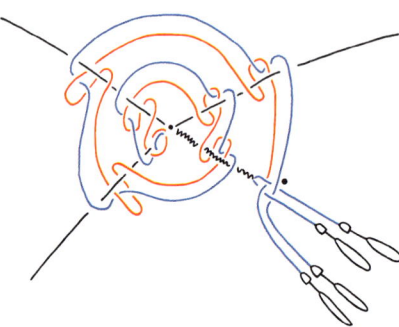

3. The first 2 times round are worked without twists on the "spider pair". Add twists to the "spider pair" on the following rounds, one extra twist for each round. The number of rounds is up to you, depending on the size of spider you want. They don't all have to be the same size. When the spider is the correct size, the twisted pair (= 4) and the "spider pair" continue in a plait. Place a support pin to keep the spider nice, round shape.

Russian tape lace filling

The filling is worked in rows, vertically or horizontally, as indicated on the pattern.

For example
Start at the green start symbol. Follow the red line and put a pin in all the crossing points – here shown as black dots on the pricking. In this case you sew in quite fast by putting the needle under the plait – not into it. The first stitch after a sewing is a whole stitch. Pull tight and work a tight plait. Continue to the next row of the pattern. At the dotted line, the plait runs along at the top of the edge stitch, if too long a stretch – sew in half way. Now work the blue line and sew in the black dots – remember the picots.

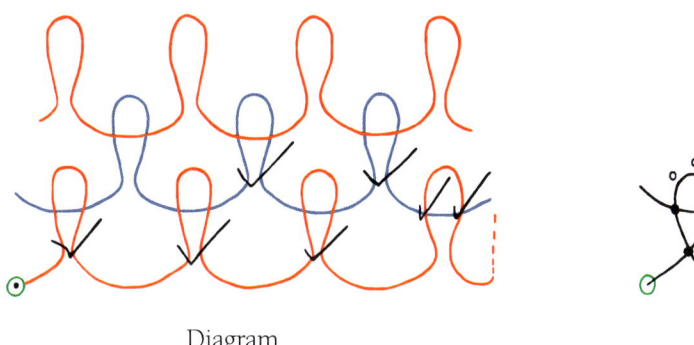 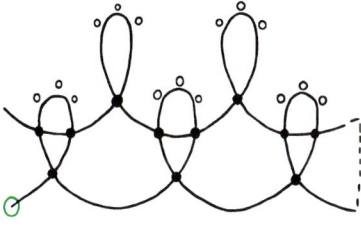

Diagram   Pricking

If the filling has a centre – sew in the last time you pass the centre – or the last time you pass a join. Only make one sewing.
It is important to make tight plaits to make a good, firm filling and, not least, that the plaits are neither too short nor too long.

The best way to work a filling is to start at one point and having worked the filling, return to the same point to finish off.

A roll of half hitches
If the distance from one row to another is too big, you can work 3-4 half hitches and cut the treads. Start again where convenient. A small "roll" of half hitches is less visible than a long plait - especially with the thick threads. Don't remove the pins before starching.

17

Adding beads to your lace

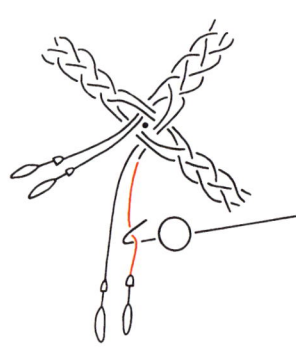
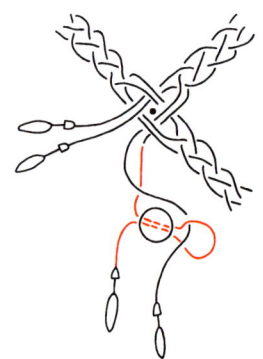
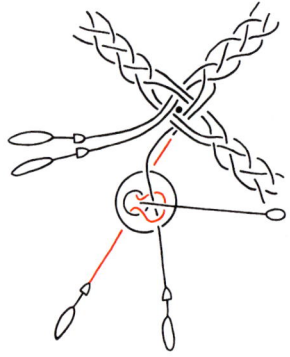

1. To get a firm centre, work some of the plait without the bead. Place the bead on the crochet hook and draw the nearest thread from the plait through the bead, making a loop.

2. Put the second bobbin from the pair through the loop.

3. Pull tight. Put a pin through the bead from the side of the loop and into the pillow to control the bead.

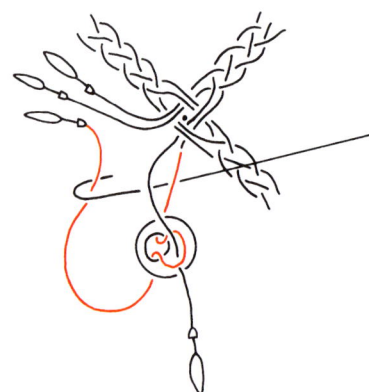

4. Pull a loop out under both threads between the bead and the windmill crossing.

5. Put the second bobbin from the pair through the loop from the top.

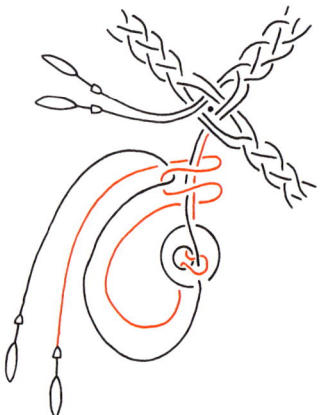

6. Pull the loop tight between the bead and the windmill crossing. Replace the pair and continue plaiting with a whole stitch.

7. The finished result.

18

Technical drawings for cone No. 12

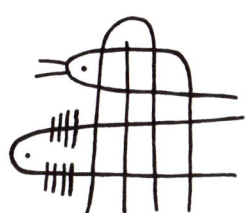

Start the narrow tape as shown here.

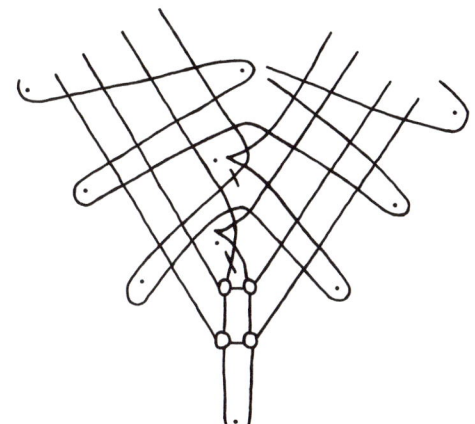

Shown here are the points of the narrow tapes.

Detail drawing.
A ring means C – T – C – T – C.

The joining of 3 or 4 loops at the same point.

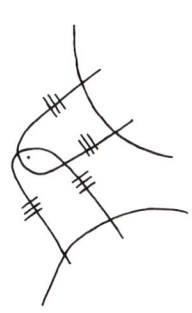

1. The 2 first loops are placed around the pin.

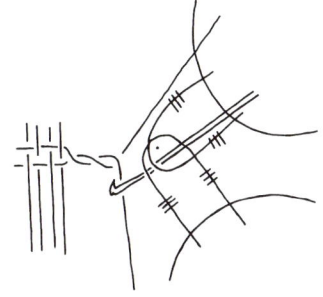

2. Third time you get to the pin you sew in THROUGH both loops.

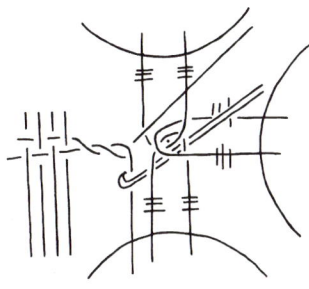

3. Fourth time you get to the point you sew UNDER all 3 loops

Cone No. 1 – Russian Tape Lace

Materials
7 pairs of linen 60/2
2 pairs of gold thread equivalent to linen 60/2 or Moravia 80/2 wound double

The 2 gold pairs work the chain stitches.
The twists and sew in marks apply for the entire piece.
Start as indicated and follow the diagram.
Remember to remove the pin after the turning stitch and pull the pairs.(p. 9)
You can complete the lace using magic threads and tie off with knots.

The Filling
The filling is plaited. Follow the arrows.
The plait runs along the edge, where indicated by a broken line (sew in half way if needed).
2 more pairs are added for the middle line.
2 plaits cross with a windmill crossing, p.11.
One of the plaits continues working the second half of the cone.
Now work the flower in the centre. Add 3 × 2 pairs as shown in the diagram, work the flower. After the 5th leaf, sew into the centre flower and then work the last leaf. Tie of the pairs as shown on p. 17, roll of half hitches.
The filling for the second half of the cone is worked in the opposite direction.

The Handle
7 pairs of linen 60/2
The full length of the handle is 17 cm.

To Finish
The lace is starched very firmly.
Stitch the cone together and end by stiching a false plait with needle and thread.
The handle is stitched on.

To work this cone in linen 16/2, set the copier at 195%.

Pricking for Cone No. 1

Diagram for Cone No. 1

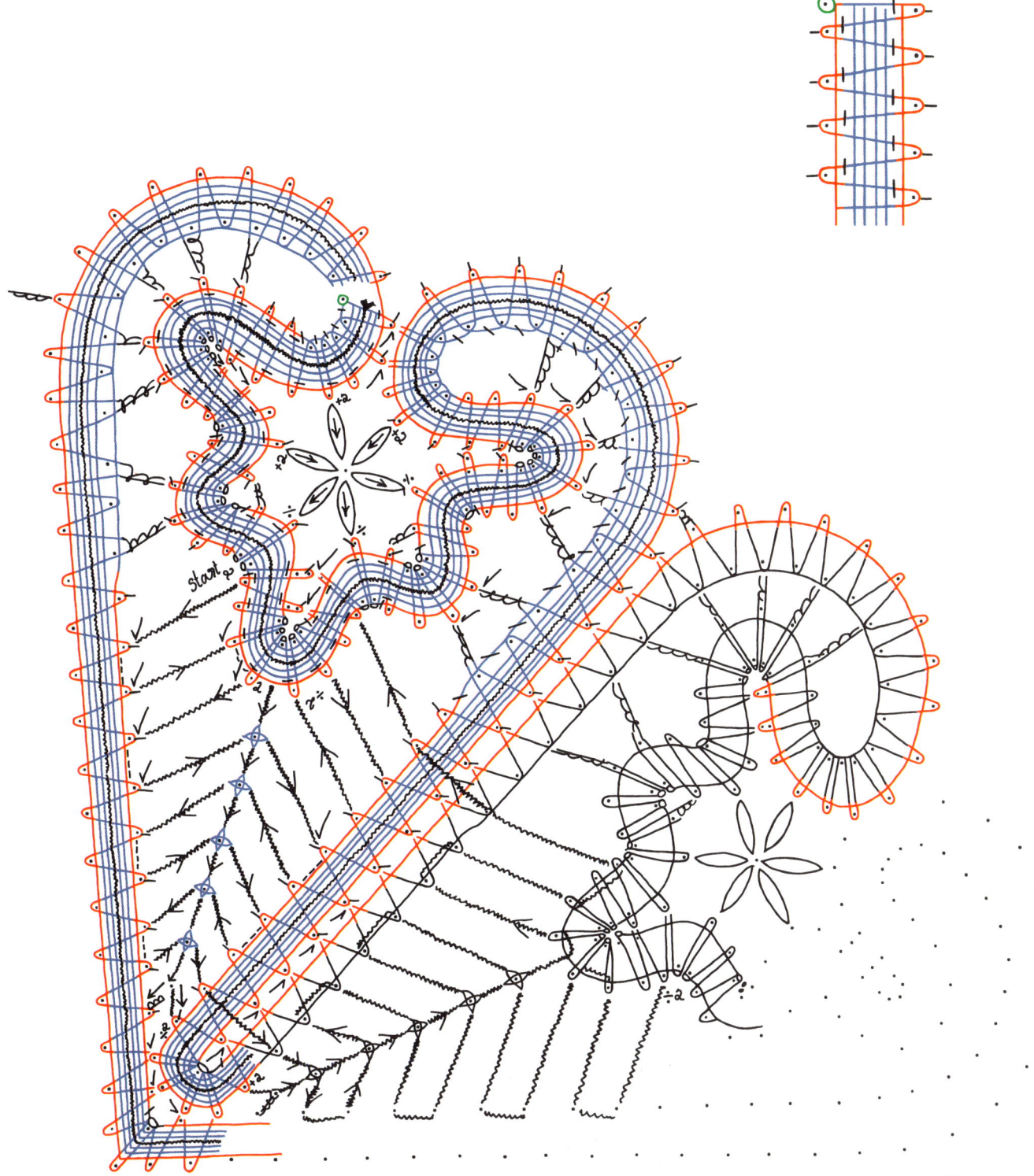

Cone No. 2 – Russian Tape Lace

Materials
7 pairs of linen 60/2
2 pairs of gold thread equivalent to linen 60/2 or Moravia 80/2 wound double

The 2 gold pairs are worked as chain stitches .
The twists and sew in marks apply for the entire piece.
Start as indicated and follow the diagram.
Remember to remove the pin after the turning stitch and pull the pairs, p. 9.
You can complete the lace using helping threads or tying off with knots.

The Filling
The filling is plaited. Follow the arrows.
The plait runs along the edge, where indicated by a broken line (sew in half way if needed).
2 new pairs are added and continue to work the filling on the right side. These 2 pairs continue working in the other half of the cone. Now work the flower in the centre. Add 3x2 pairs as shown on the diagram, work the flower and tie the pairs off as shown on p. 17. After the 5th leaf sew in to make the flower and then work the last leaf. The filling for the second half of the cone is worked in the opposite direction.

The Handle
7 pairs of linen 60/2
2 pairs of gold or silver thread for the chain stitches
The full length of the handle is 21 cm.

To Finish
The lace is starched very firmly.
Stitch the cone together and end by stiching a false plait with needle and thread.
Stitch on the handle.

To work this cone in linen 16/2, set the copier at 195%.

Pricking for Cone No. 2

Diagram for Cone No. 2

Cone No. 3
– Russian Tape Lace

Materials
7 pairs of linen 60/2
2 pairs of DMC silver thread art. 283 equivalent to linen 35/2

The 2 silver pairs are worked as chain stitches.
The twists and sew in marks apply for the entire piece.
Start as indicated on the diagram.
Remember to add an extra twist to the workers where you will sew in later.
NB the 3 false plaits marked ⚏ and the change of the edge.
Sew in and tie off.

The Filling
12 pairs of linen 60/2

The plaited filling takes 12 pairs. 2 plaits cross in a windmill crossing, p. 11.
Follow the diagram.

The Handle
7 pairs of linen 60/2
2 pairs of DMC silver thread article 283 equivalent to linen 35/2
The full length of the handle is 21 cm.

The 2 silver pairs are worked as chain stitches.

To Finish
The lace is starched very firmly.
Stitch the cone together.
Stitch on the handle.

Pricking for Cone No. 3

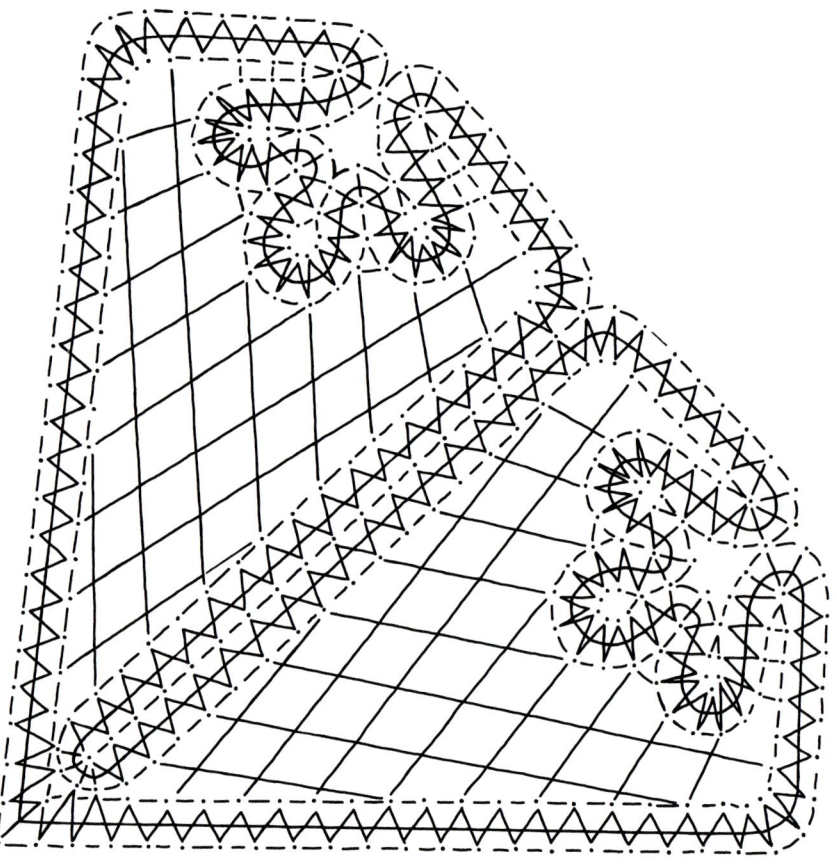

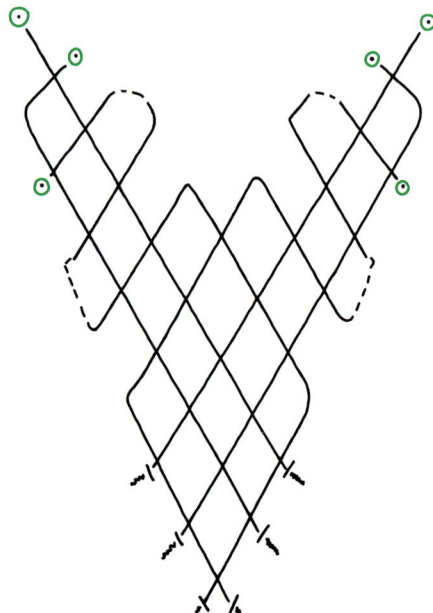

Diagram for Cone No. 3

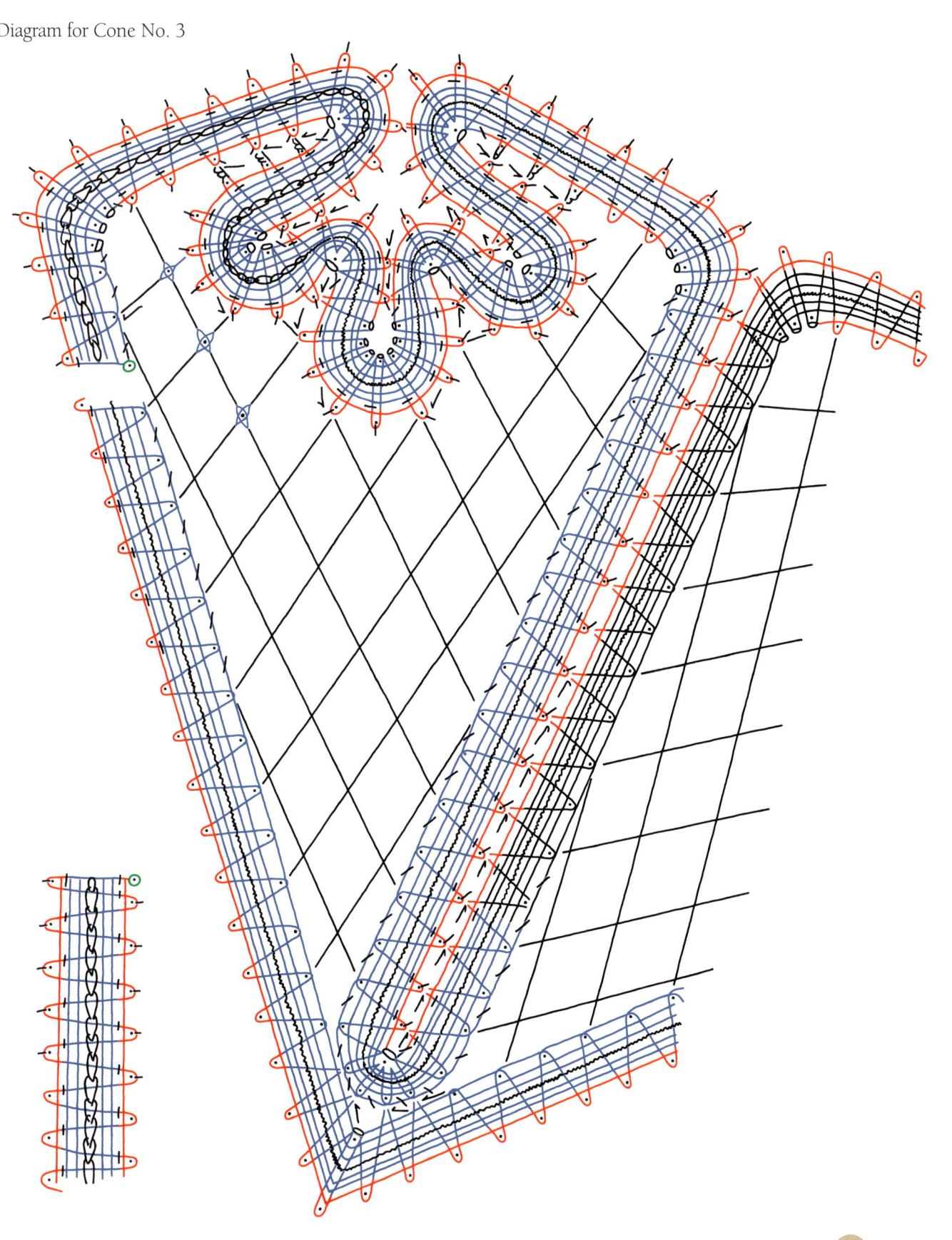

Cone No. 4 – Czech inspired

Materials
19 pairs of linen 40/2 e.g. from Moravia
2 pairs of DMC gold art. 282
Approx. 16 pearls, 3mm gold
Goldpainted wallpaper for the point of the cone

It is very difficult to work a nice point in lace. That is why I have made a small cone in wallpaper for the point. Wallpaper or some other good quality paper is exellent for the purpose.
Start the lace at A with 3 pairs of linen – then the 2 gold pairs. From one of the pairs at A one bobbin is a worker bobbin throughout the entire lace, and that means that the beads are threaded onto that thread. A worker bobbin in half stitch is maintained by adding an extra twist at the pins. This also means that you have to wind extra thread onto that bobbin. The beads are pushed into position where you want them.
The lace is completed by tying off at the marked pinholes.
Each line in the diagram = 1 bobbin in halfstitch – other pairs are tied off in pairs.

The Handle
7 pairs of linen 40/2
2 pairs of DMC gold
The full length of the handle is 23 cm.

To Finish
The lace is starched very firmly.
Place the starting loops on top of the knots and stitch the cone together with a thin thread. Stitch on the handle.

Cut a cone point from the template, colour it gold or bronze and glue.

Pricking for Cone No. 4

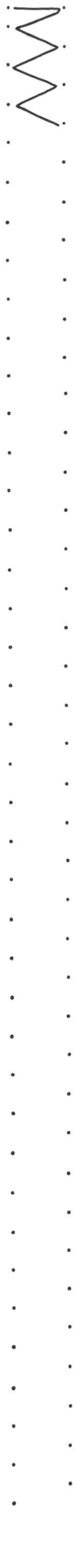

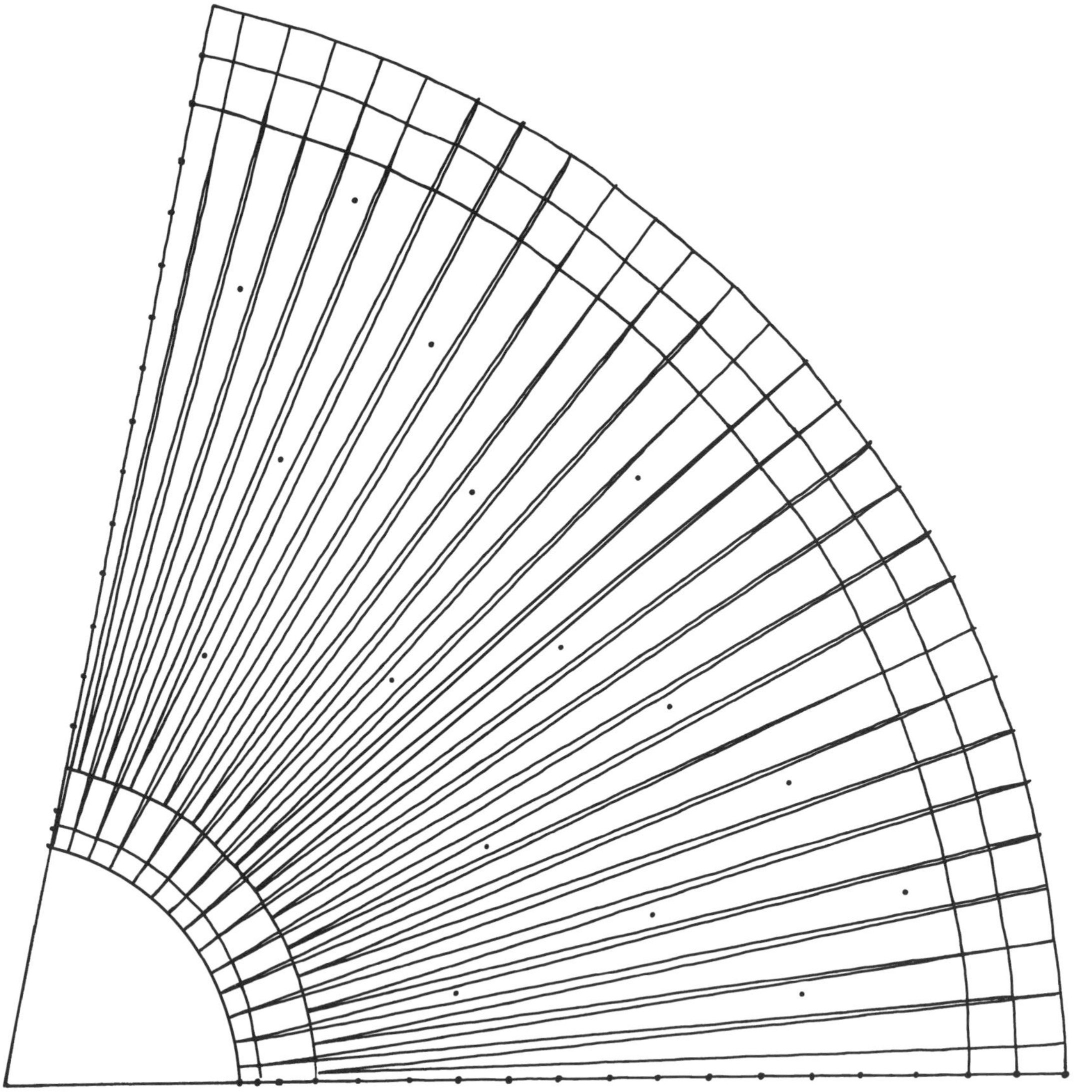

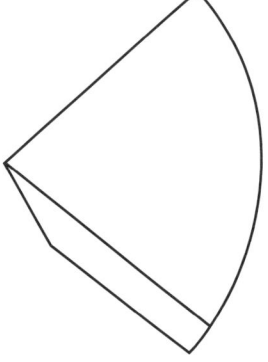

Diagram for Cone No. 4

○ linen thread
● gold- or silver thread
● beads

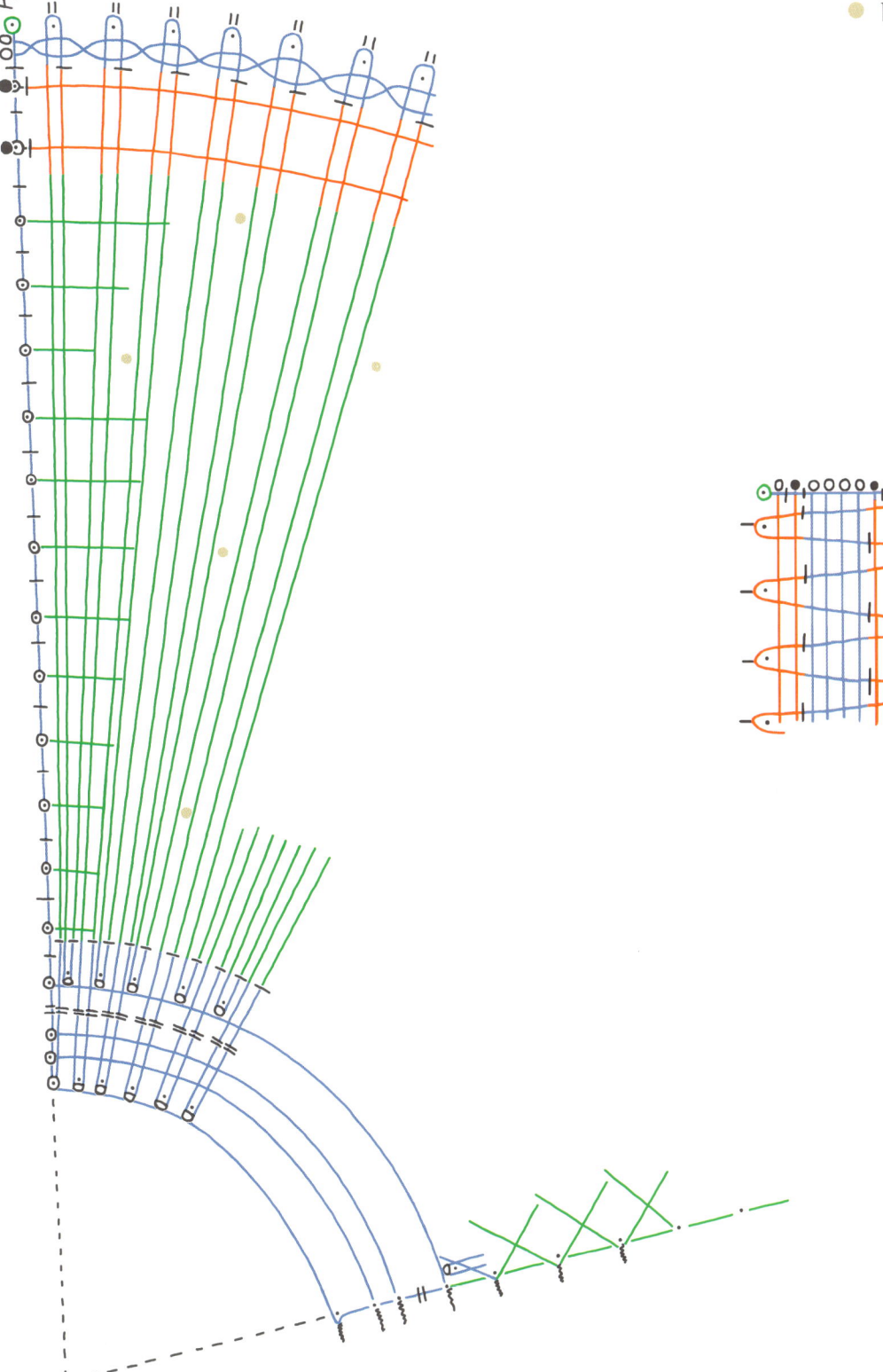

Cone No. 5 – Czech inspired

Materials
31 pairs of linen 40/2 e.g. from Moravia
4 pairs of DMC gold art. 282
Goldpainted wallpaper for the point of the cone

Start the first band at A with 13 pairs of linen + 4 pairs of gold.
Work 2 pairs in whole stitch (CTC) – 7 pairs in half stitch (CT) – 1 pair whole stitch and a twist (CTCT) + 5 pairs worked as contour stitches (see diagram) – the outer pair as a turning stitch, p. 9.
Follow the diagram. The pairs are tied off with 2-3 reef-knots.
The next band is started at B. 18 pairs are worked and sewn into the first tape. Use the "raised sewing" technique, p. 9.
The whole stitch bottom band is ended in pairs as shown on p. 17, roll of half hitches. The half stitches are knottet off with 3 reef knots.
Each line at the diagram = 1 bobbin in halfstitch.

The Handle
9 pairs of linen 40/2
2 pairs of DMC gold
The full length of the handle is 23 cm.

The handle is worked with whole stitch and a twist at both sides and the worker goes through 8 pairs as a contour thread as shown on the diagram.

To Finish
The lace is starched very firmly.
Place the starting loops on top of the knots and stitch the cone together with a thin thread.
Stitch on the handle.

Cut a cone point from the template, colour it gold or bronze and glue.

Pricking for Cone No. 5

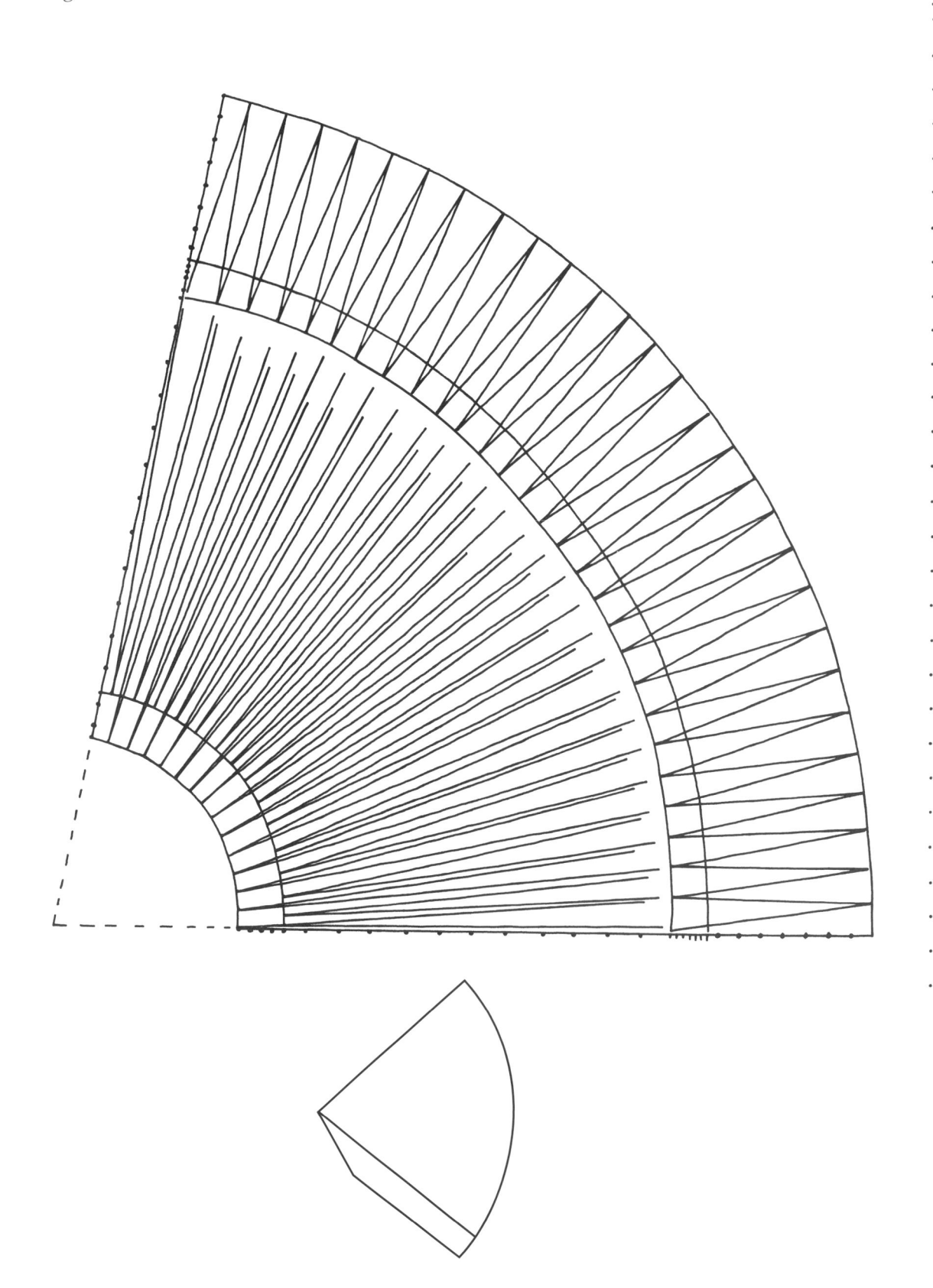

Diagram for Cone No. 5

○ linen thread
● gold- or silver thread

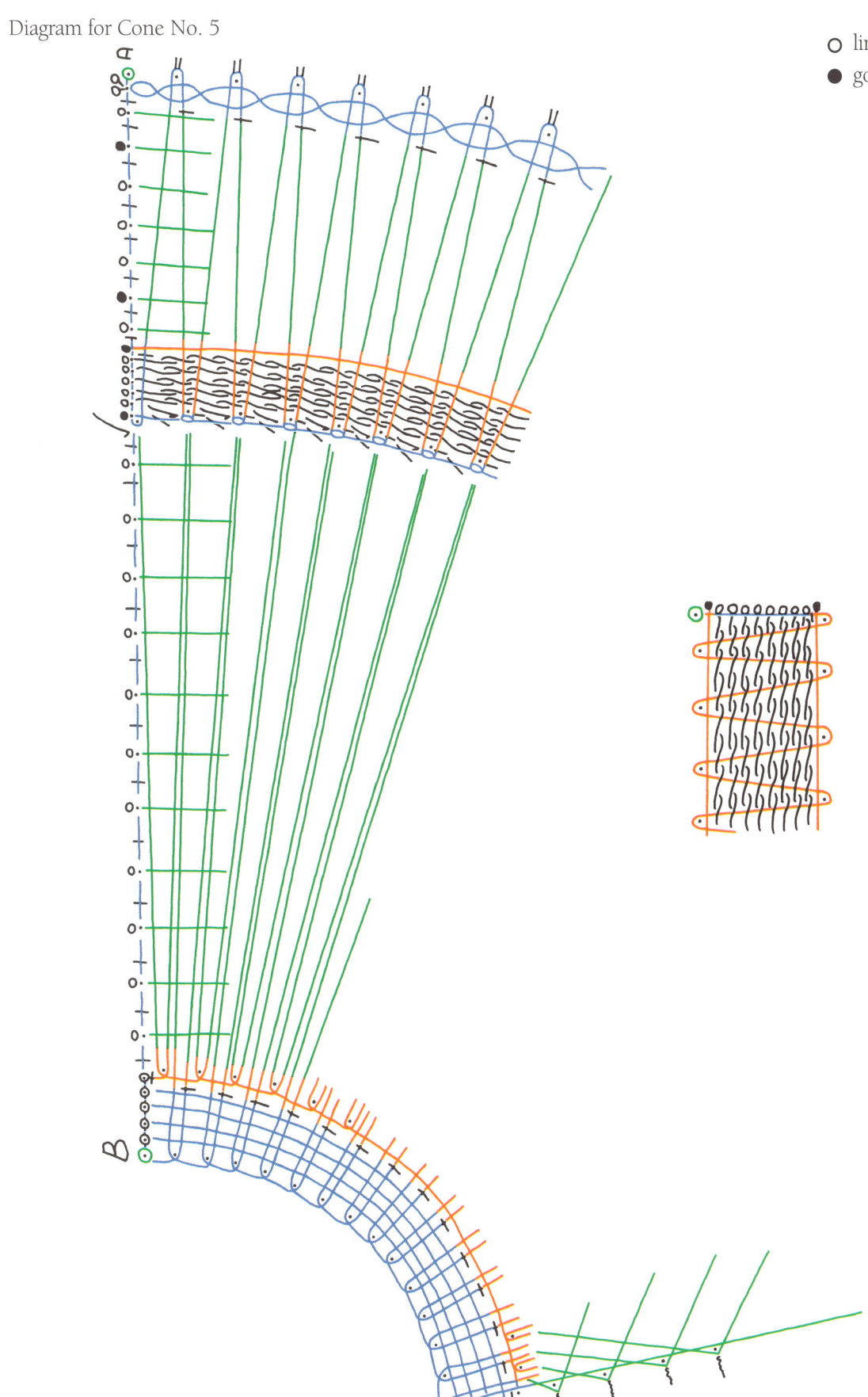

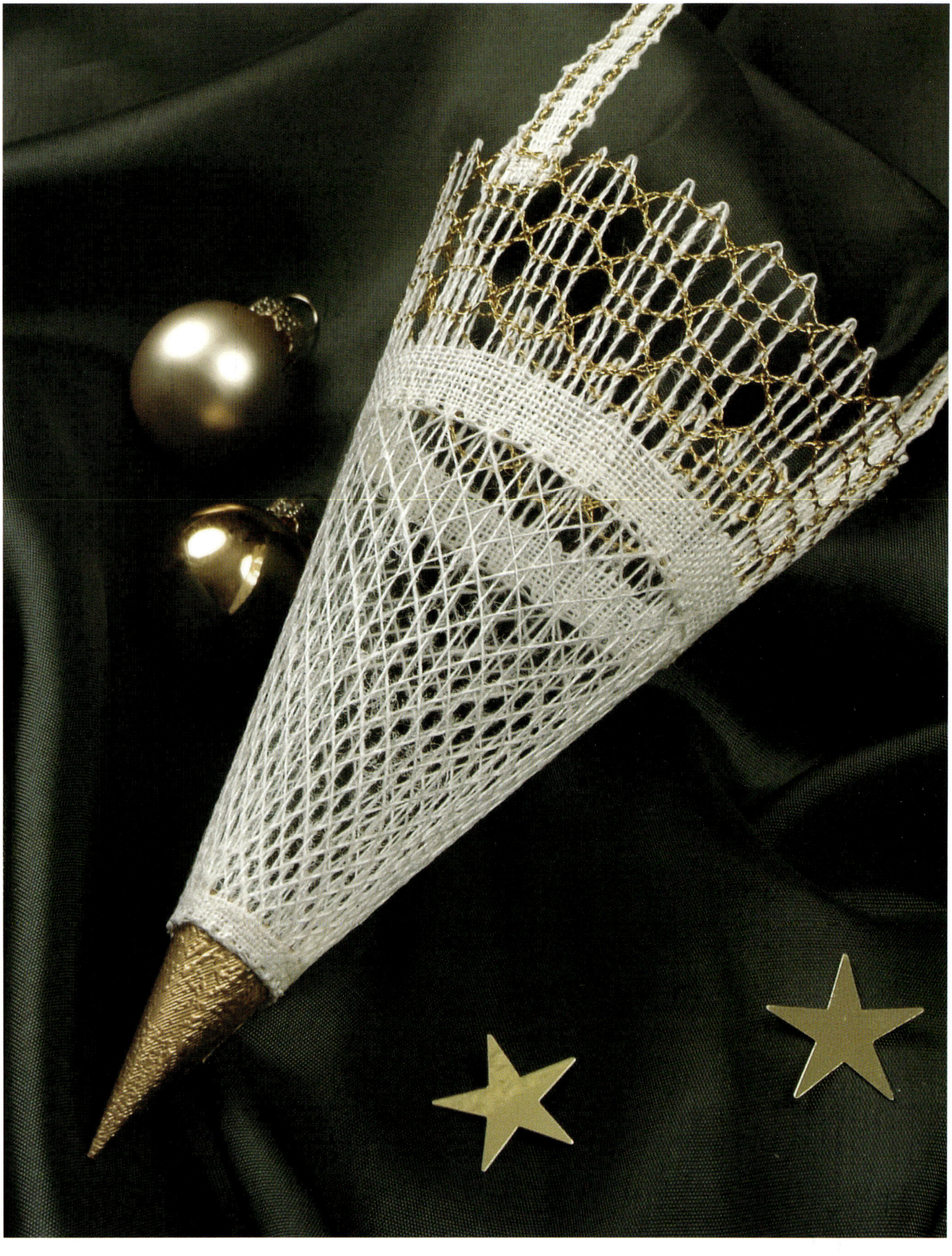

Cone No. 6
– Czech inspired

Materials
23 pairs of linen 40/2 e.g. from Moravia
6 pairs of DMC gold art. 282 or silver art. 283
Goldpainted wallpaper for the point of the cone

Start no. 1: The first band starts at A with 7 pairs of linen and 6 pairs of metallic thread. The metallic pairs work a whole stitch with a twist and a pin is placed in the middle of the stitch. Follow the diagram to continue. At the end the linen threads are knotted off, but the metallic threads must be left. DON'T STARCH THEM – they will be sewn into the starting loops and tied off when you stitch the cone together with a needle.

Start no. 2: 1 pair is sewn in at A and the rest of the pairs are worked in with it – 16 pairs all together.
Continue following the diagram. The half stitches are sewn in to the first band.
When tying off use the pinholes. A line on the diagram is one bobbin in half stitch. To finish the whole stitch band, tie off in pairs.

The Handle
7 pairs of linen 40/2
2 pairs of DMC gold or silver
The full length of the handle is 23 cm.

To Finish
The lace is starched very firmly.
The ends of the metallic threads are sewn in to the starting loops and are tied off with a reef knot.
Place the starting loops on top of the knots and stitch the cone together with a thin thread. Remember to starch the stitching.
Stitch on the handle.

Cut a cone point from the template, colour it gold or bronze and glue.

Pricking for Cone No. 6

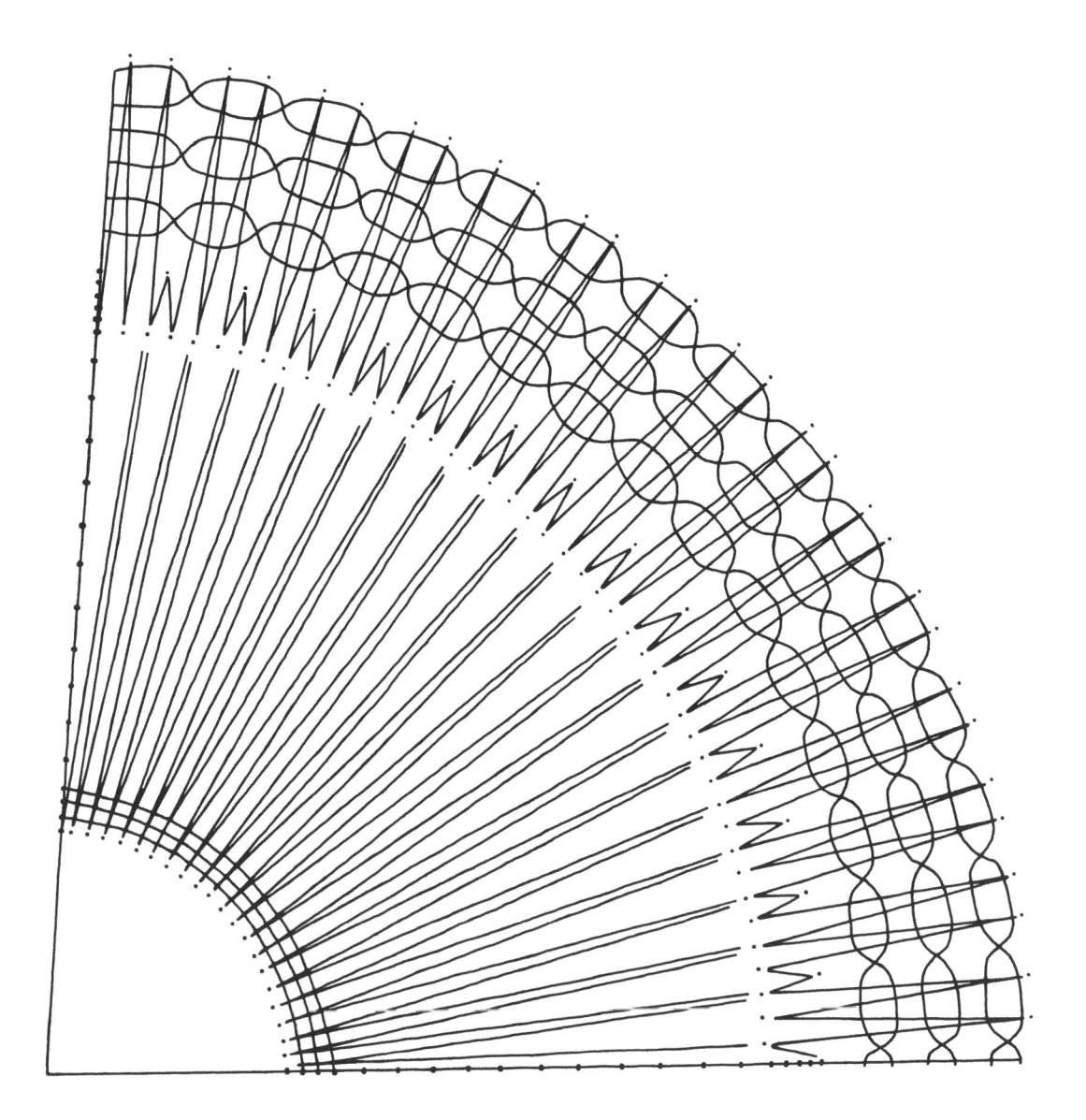

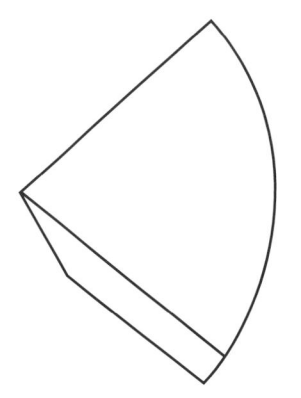

Diagram for Cone No. 6

○ linen thread
● gold- or silver thread

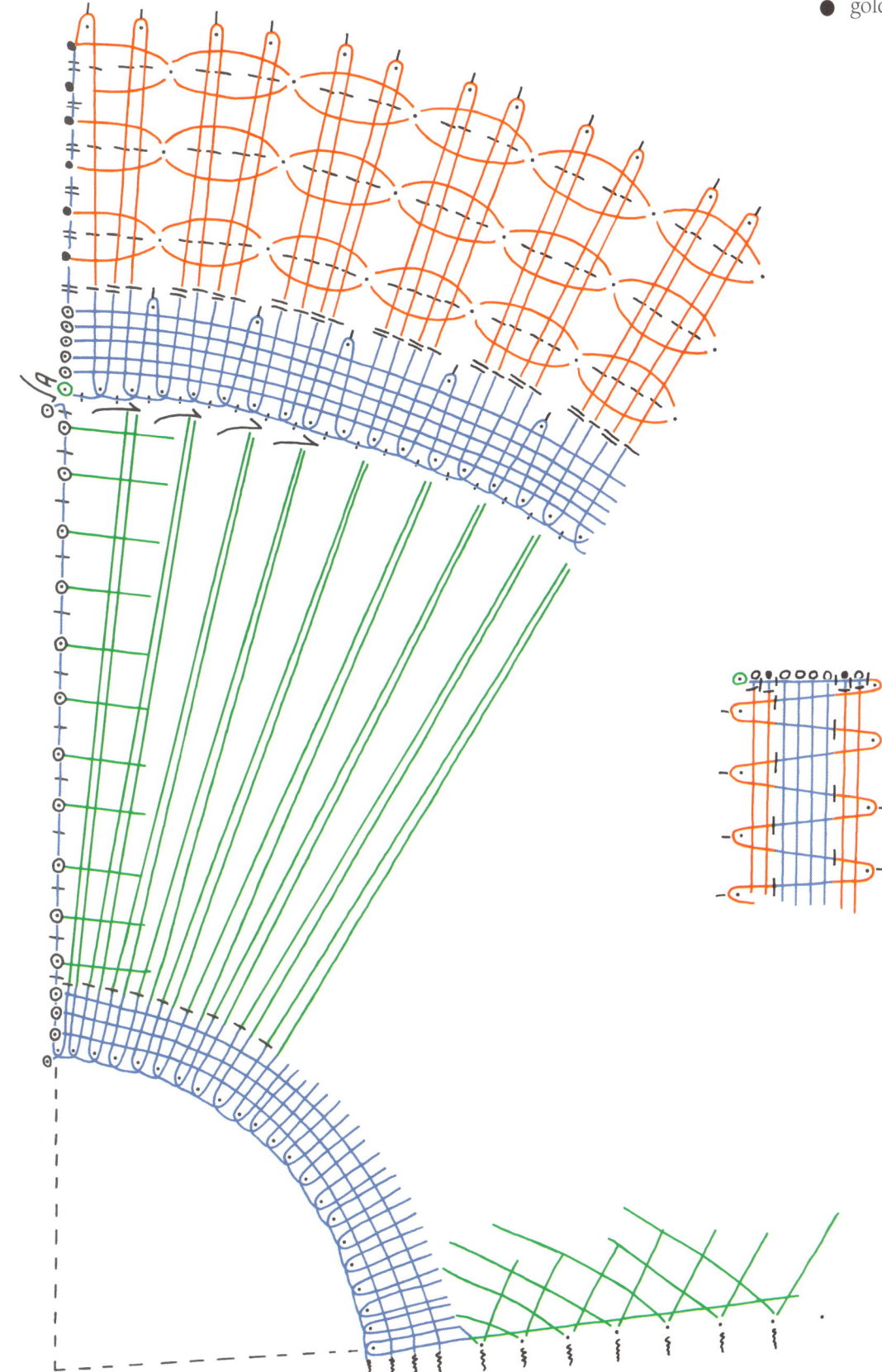

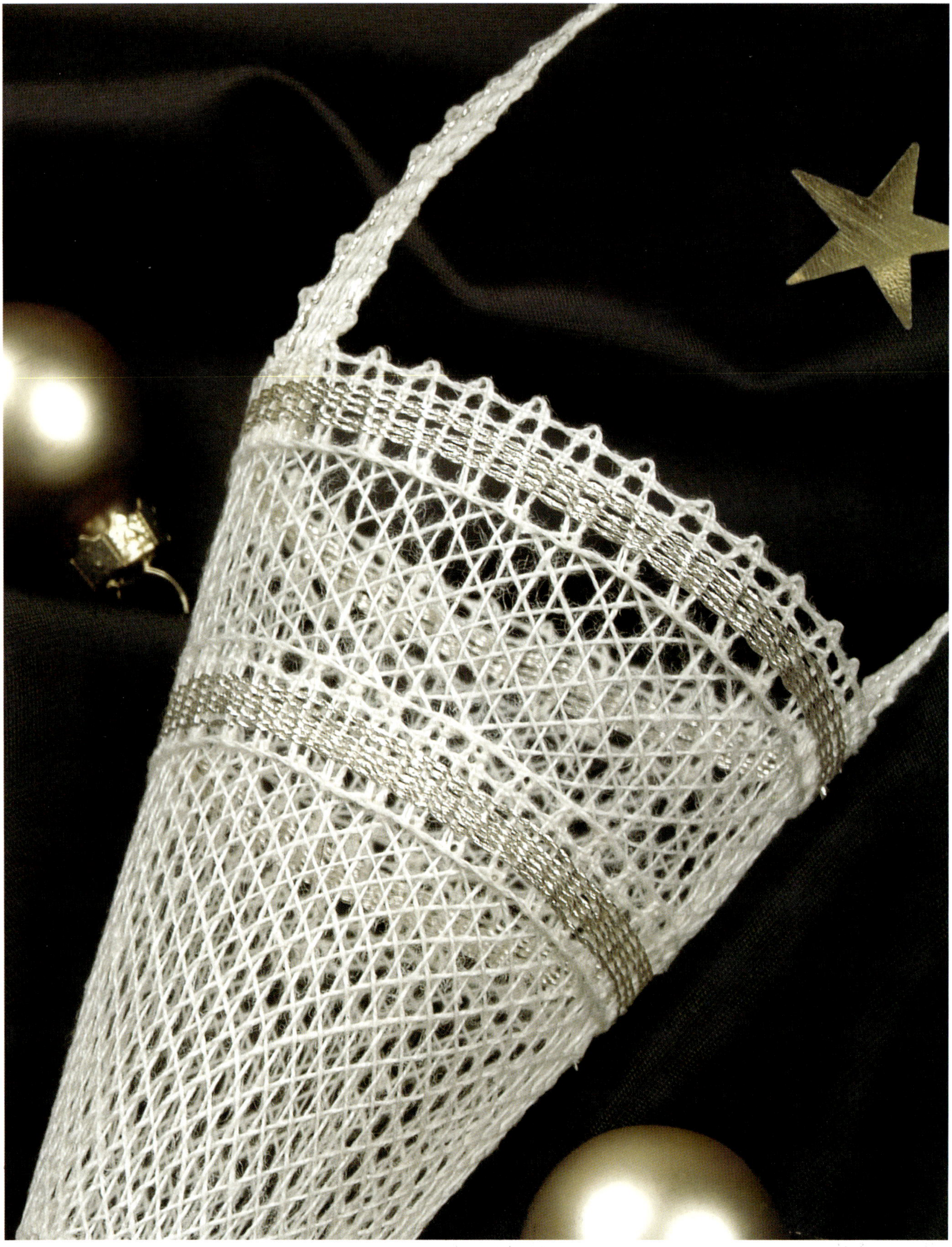

Cone No. 7
– Czech inspired

Materials
Swedish linen 40/2 or from Moravia
DMC metallic silver art. 283

Start band 1 at A with 3 pairs of linen, 6 pairs of silver and 2 pairs of linen of which one is the worker.. Let the first worker from A run all the way along the side of the cone. All the other pairs are worked into it. Finish the first band. All the silver pairs are worked as contour stitches – see diagram. The pairs are tied off with 2-3 reef knots. Then work 5 linen pairs up to the starting edge and leave them to one side. Complete band 2.

The Filling
The filling between the two bands is worked in half stitch. Note that one more pair is sewn in. Use the raised sewing technique, p. 9.
When you tie off in half stitch you use the pins to tie around. Make 2-3 reef knots.
Now work band no. 3. Finish it and work the half stitch filling between bands 2 and 3. Finish the point of the cone by working turn stitch (p.9) and a single whole stitch.
3 pairs are joined at x. Take 5 of the 6 threads and make roll of half hitches, p.17. The 6th bobbin continues to the half stitches and is crossed with a bobbin from these – is tied off with 2-3 reef knots etc. One line is one bobbin.

The Handle
8 pairs of linen 40/2
2 pairs of DMC metallic silver art. 283
The full length of the handle is 23 cm.

The handle is worked with whole stitch with a twist in both sides, 7 gimp pairs as contour stitches.

To Finish
The lace is starched very firmly.
Place the starting loops on top of the knots and stitch the cone together with a thin thread.
The handle is stitched on.

Pricking for Cone No. 7

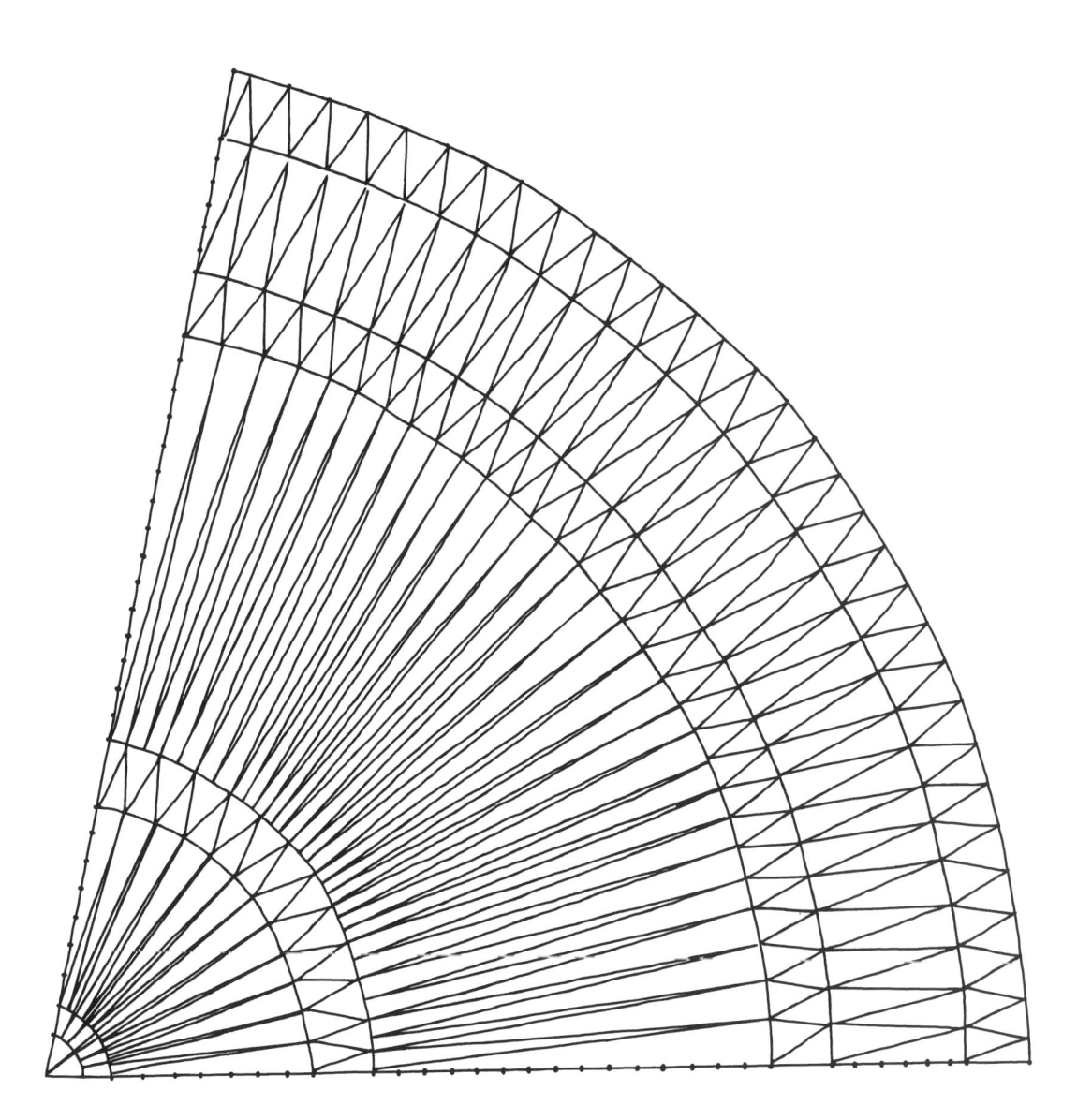

Diagram for Cone No. 7

○ linen thread
● gold- or silver thread

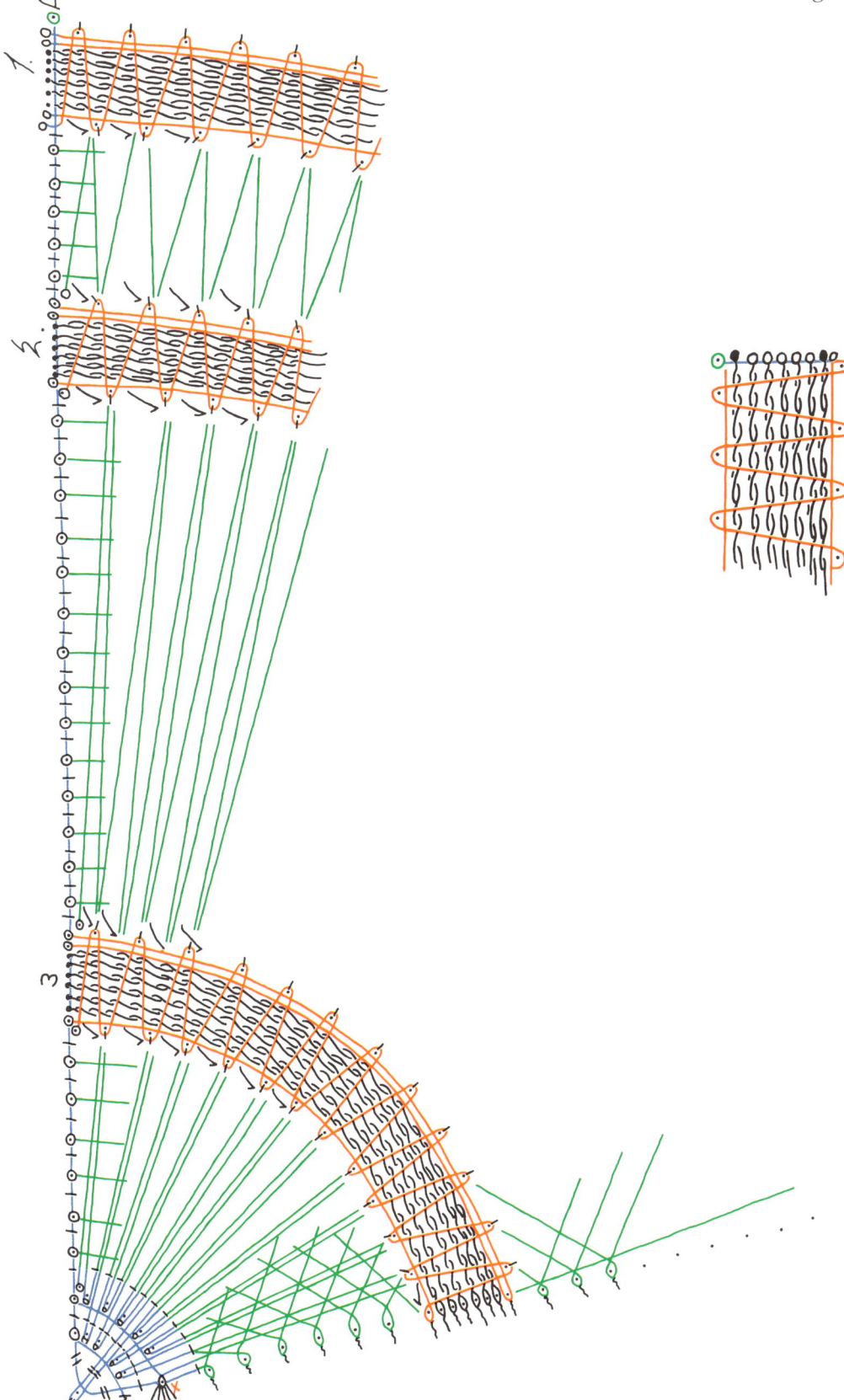

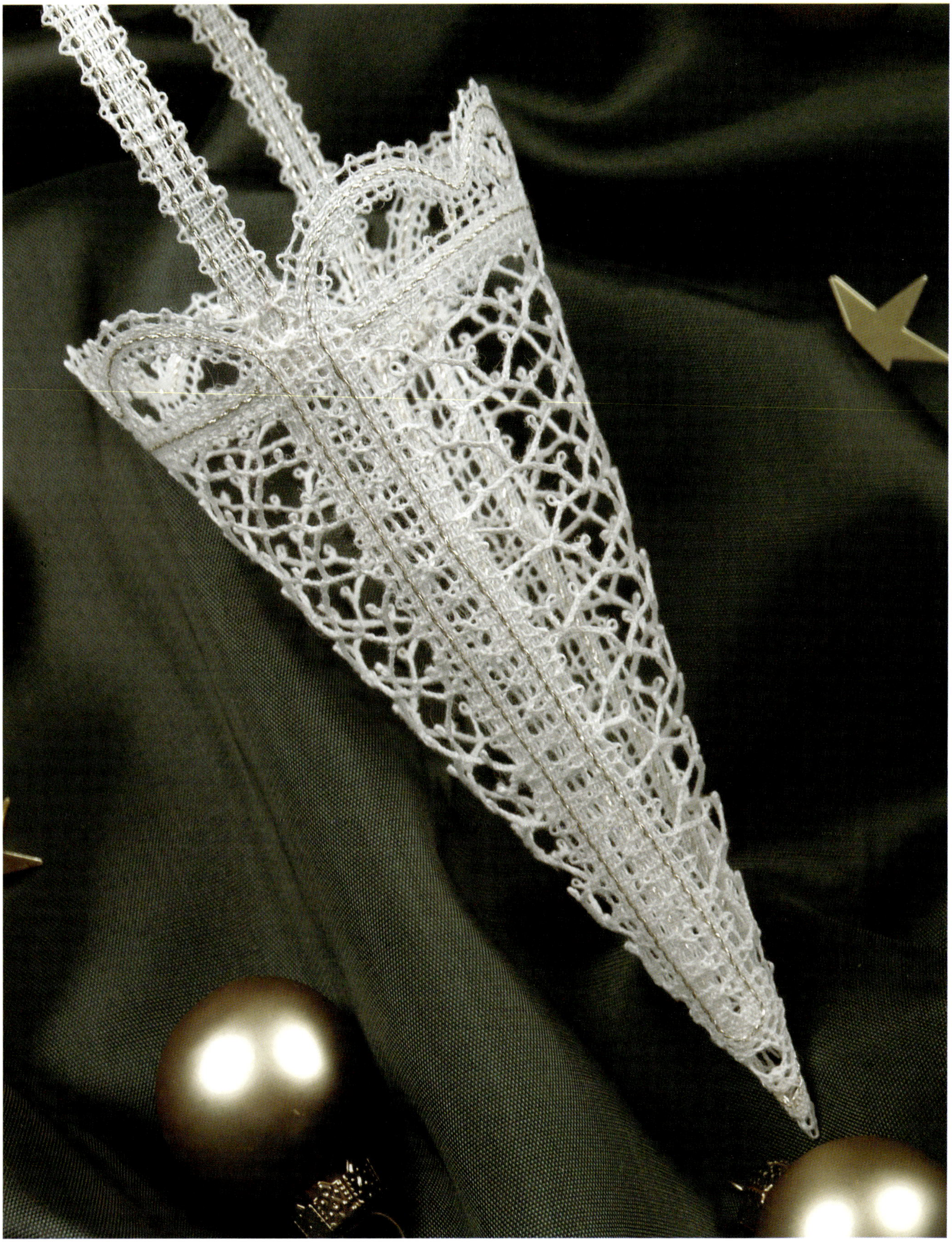

Cone No. 8 – Russian Tape Lace

Materials
7 pairs of linen 60/2
1 pair of DMC metallic thread, gold art. 282 or silver art. 283

The 2 gold or silver pairs are worked as contour stitches.
The twists and sew in marks apply for the entire piece.

Start the tape as indicated on the diagram and work the tape all the way round. At the bottom of the cone work turn stitch and back stitch. The back stitch is marked with an x.
Finish the tape by sewing in at the starting loops and tie off with a row of knots.
If some of the bobbins have enough thread (linen), use the nearest ones for the next tape.
This tape continues into the second part of the tape (marked with a dotted line).

The Filling
Work the filling with plaits and picots. The "two threaded picot with 6 twists" on p.15 is used. Start at the bottom of the cone and follow the red line. Sew in at the edge with a raised sewing, p. 9. Work a plait and lay it along the edge and sew into the next pinhole. Now follow the blue line. Sew into the red line at the "sew in" symbol. All blue and red lines are sewn in with whole pairs, method 2, p.14. At the end work 4-5 half hitches, p.17.

The handle
7 pairs of linen 60/2
1 pairs of DMC metallic gold art. 282 or silver art. 283
The full length of the handle is 20 cm.

The gold or silver thread is worked as a contour thread.

To Finish
The lace is starched heavily; remove all support pins before starching.
Stitch the cone together loop to loop with a thinner thread e.g. linen 80/2.
Stitch on the handle.

Pricking for Cone No. 8

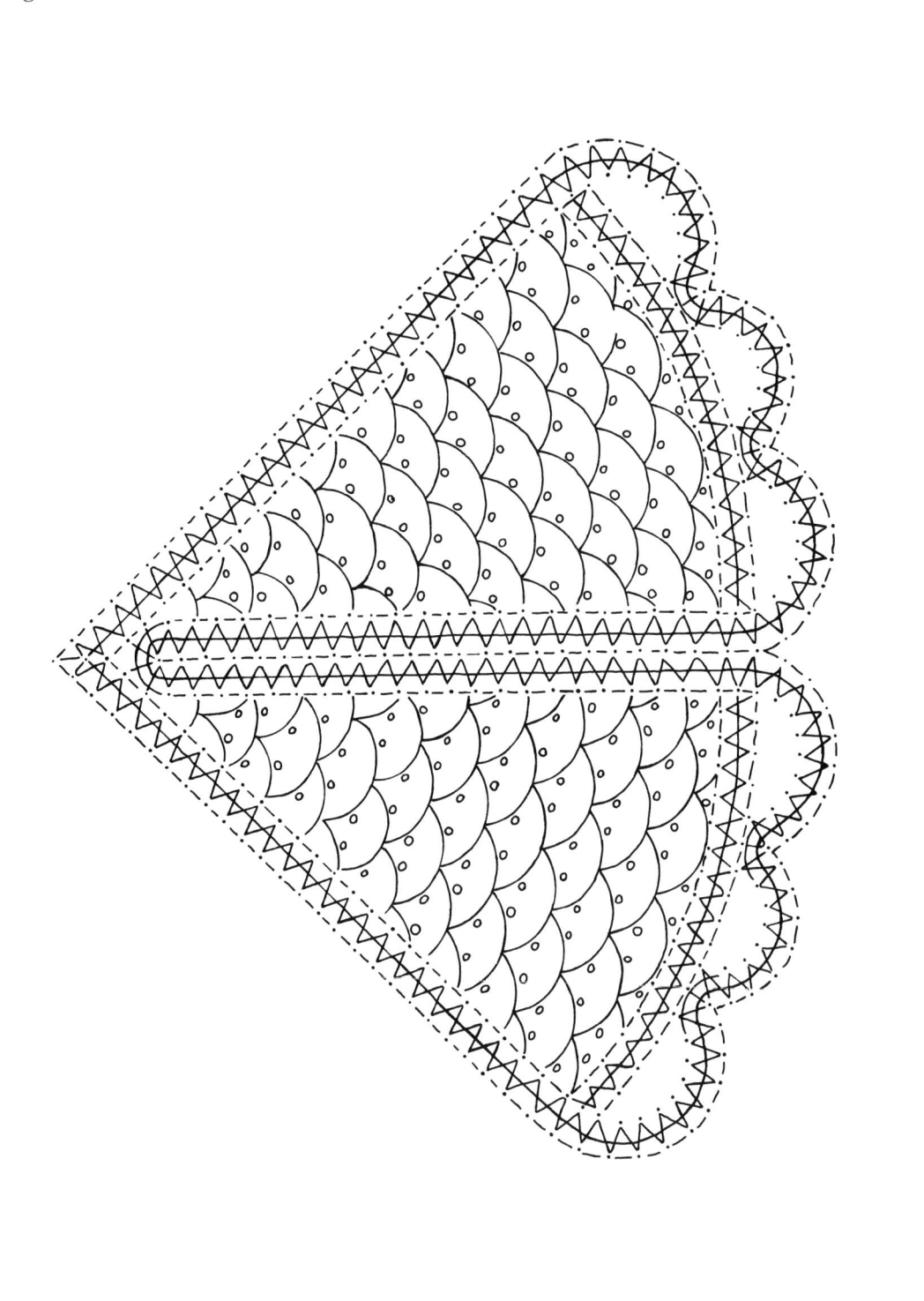

Diagram for Cone No. 8

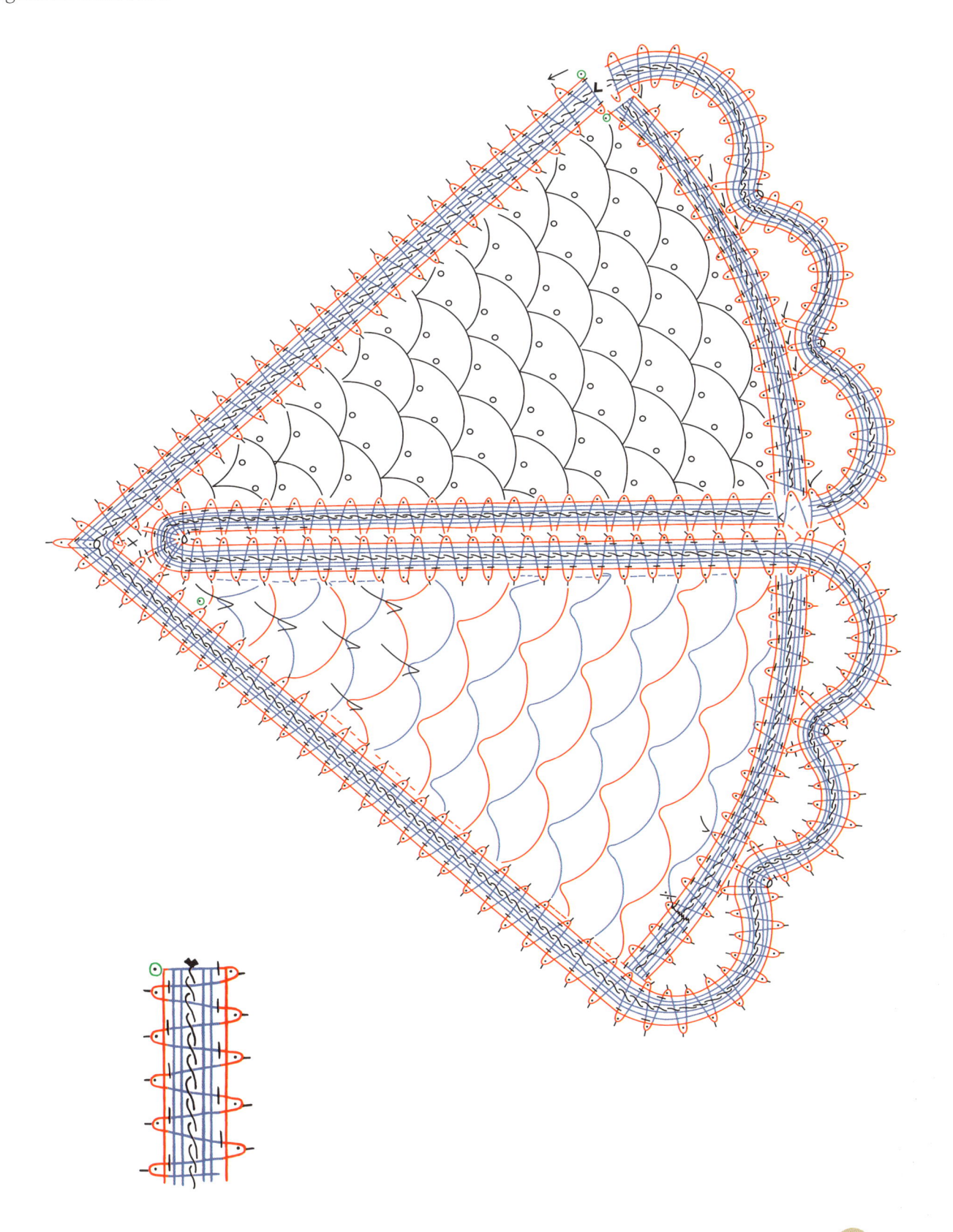

51

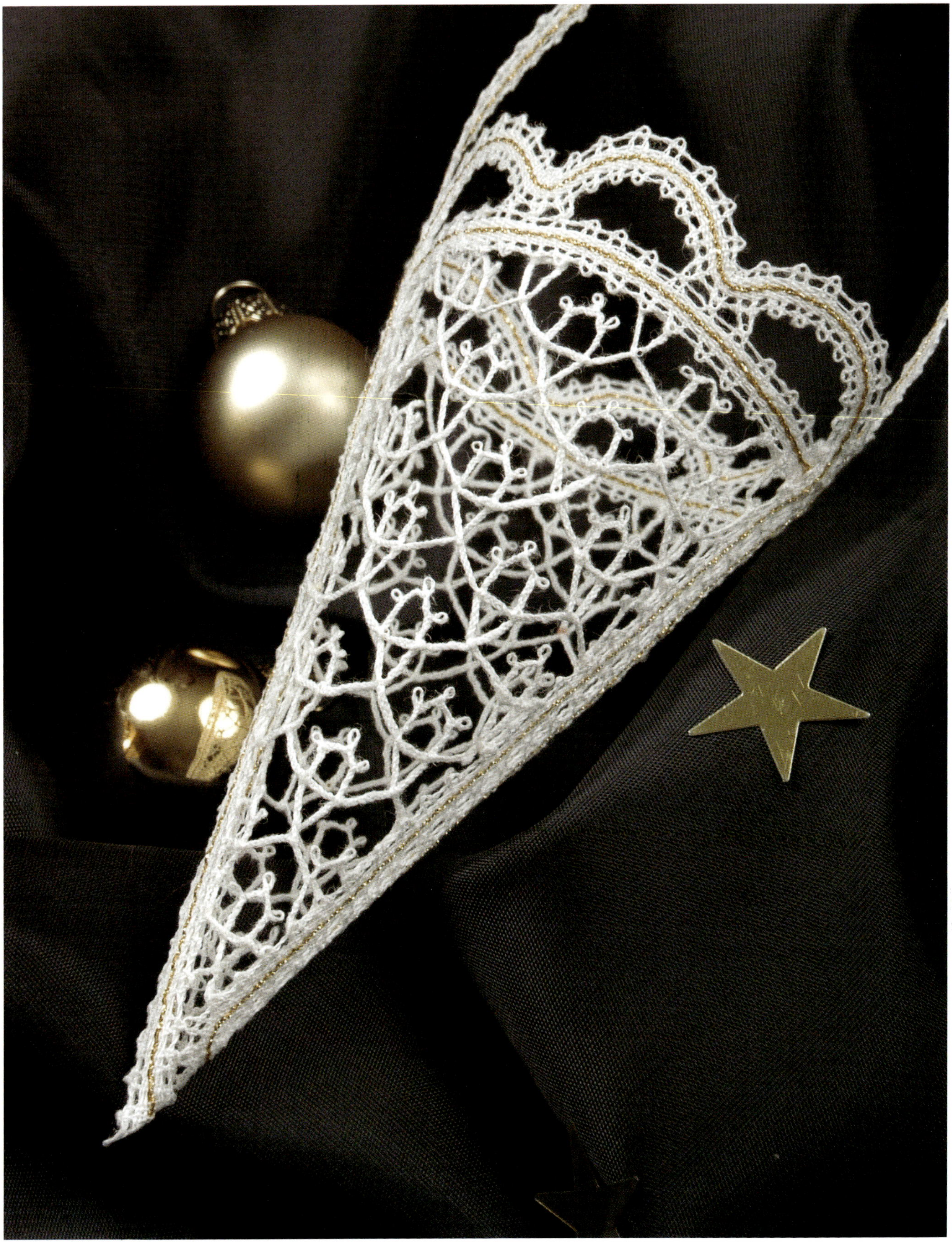

Cone No. 9 – Russian Tape Lace

Materials
7 pairs of linen 60/2
1 pair of DMC metallic thread, gold art. 282 or silver art. 283

The 2 gold or silver pairs are worked as contour stitches.
The twists and sew in marks apply for the entire piece.

Start the tape as indicated on the diagram and work the tape all the way round. At the bottom of the cone work turn stitch and back stitch. The back stitch is marked with an x.
Finish the tape by sewing in at the starting loops and tie off with a row of knots.
If some of the bobbins have enough thread (linen), use the nearest ones for the next tape.
This tape continues into the second part of the tape (marked with a dotted line).

The Filling
Work the filling according to the same principals as cone no. 8.
The sewing in is worked according to "two plaits crossing …" on p. 12.
In the ℓ curve you sew in with 2 pairs, use method 1 or 2 on page 13 or page14.
Sewing in at the edge – see p. 8.
Finish at the bottom with a small roll of half hitches, p. 17.

The Handle
7 pairs of linen 60/2
1 pairs of DMC metallic gold art. 282 or silver art. 283
The full length of the handle is 21 cm.

The gold or silver thread is worked as a contour thread.

To Finish
The lace is starched heavily; remove all support pins before starching.
Stitch the cone together loop to loop with a thinner thread e.g. linen 80/2.
Stitch on the handle.

Pricking for Cone No. 9

Diagram for Cone No. 9

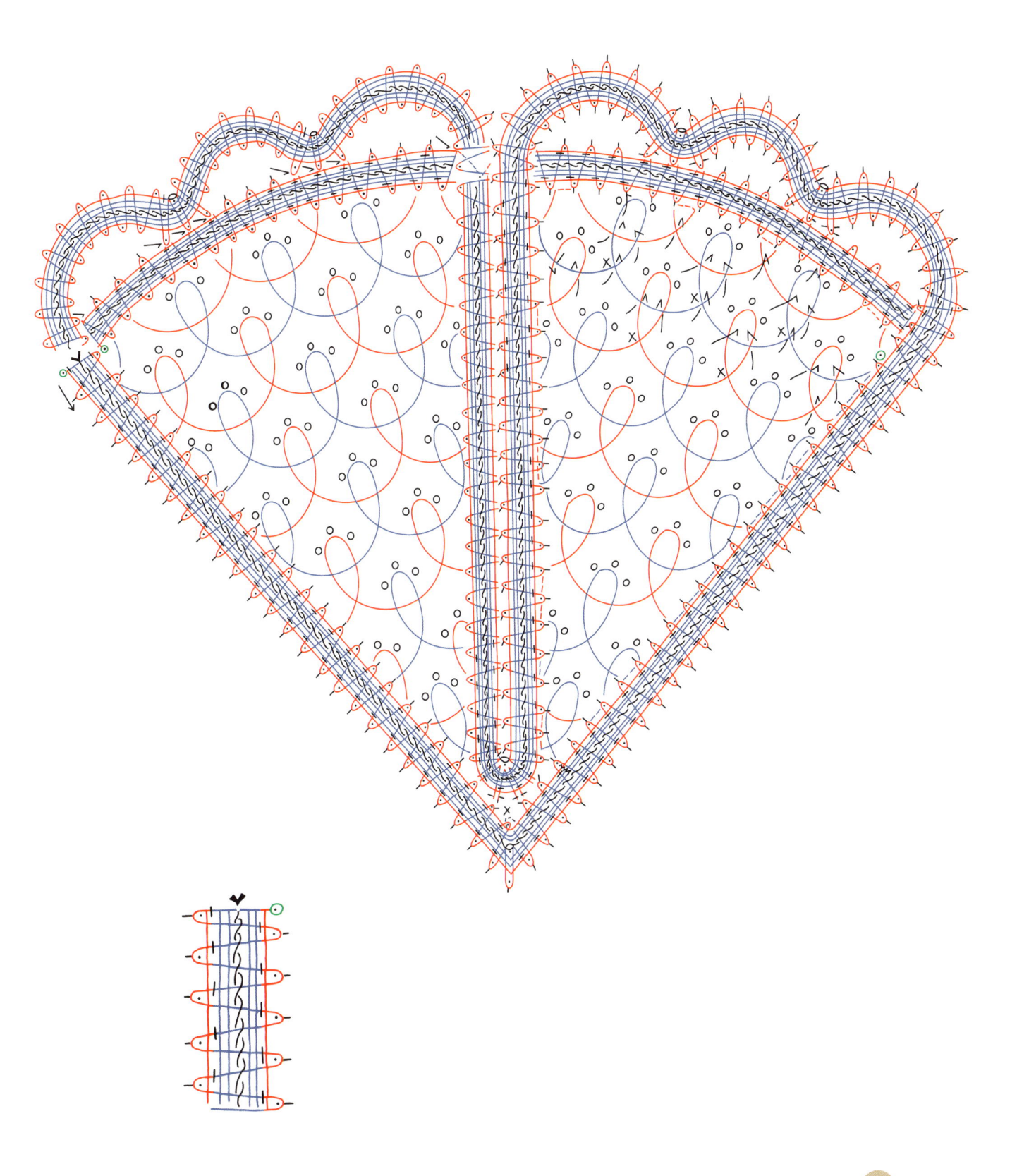

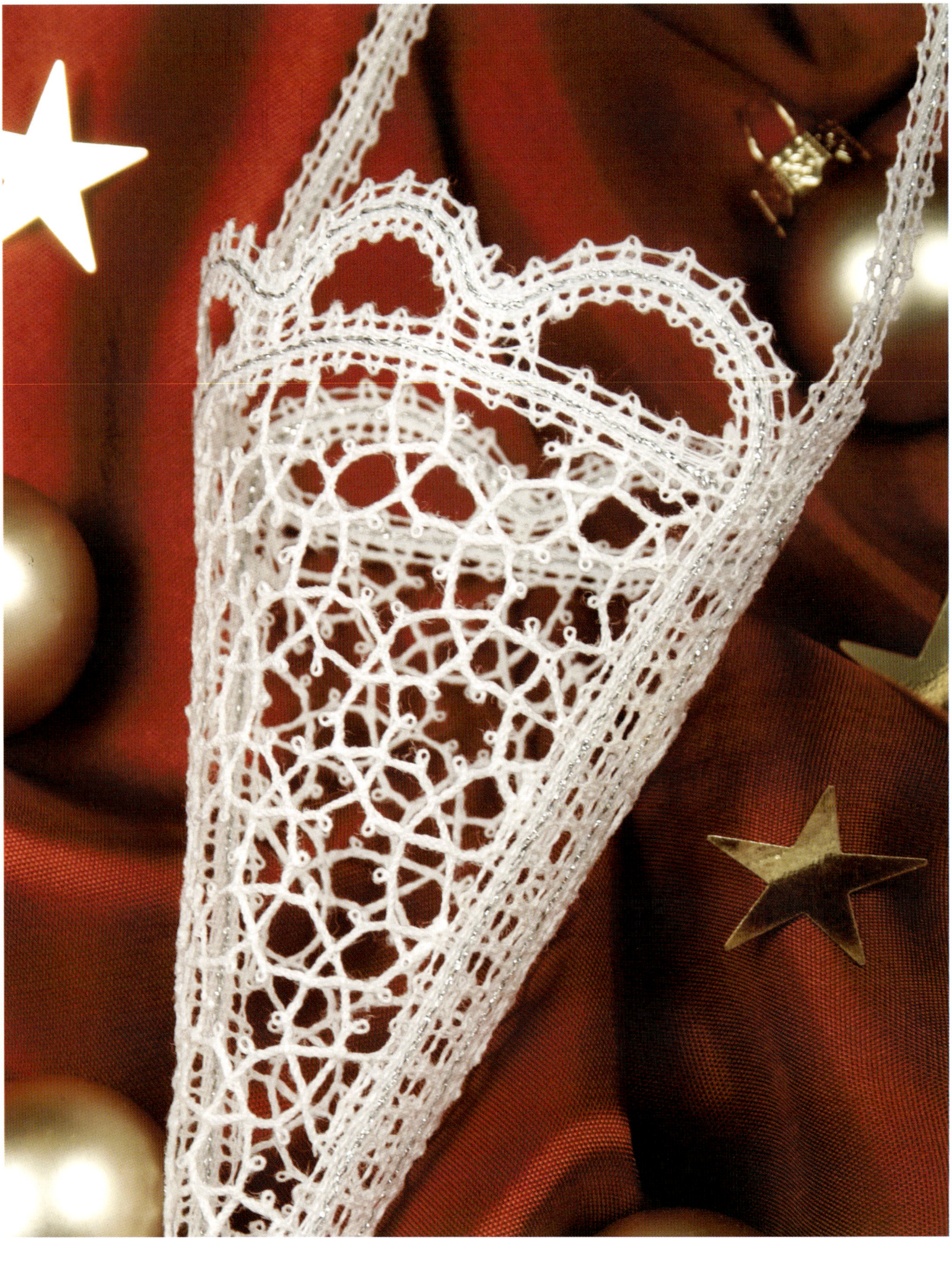

Cone No. 10 – Russian Tape Lace

Materials
7 pairs of linen 60/2
1 pair of DMC metallic thread, silver art. 283.

The silver pairs are worked as contour stitches.
The twists and sew in marks apply for the entire piece.
Start the tape at the mark and follow the diagram. The procedure is the same as for cone no. 8 and no. 9.

The Filling
The filling is plaits and picots. Use the outer pairs from the diagonal tape if they have plenty of thread. The filling is worked in horizontal rows. One way is marked in blue, the other in red. See the example on p. 17.
Tie off with a small roll of half hitches – p. 17.
The 2 curves in the top left corner (marked in black) are worked separately to avoid some very long plaits on the wrong side.

The Handle
7 pairs of linen 60/2
1 pairs of DMC metal silver art. 283
The full length of the handle is 20 cm.

The gold or silver thread is worked as a contour thread.

To Finish
The lace is starched heavily; remove all support pins before starching.
Stitch the cone together loop to loop with a thinner thread e.g. linen 80/2.
Stitch on the handle.

Pricking for Cone No. 12

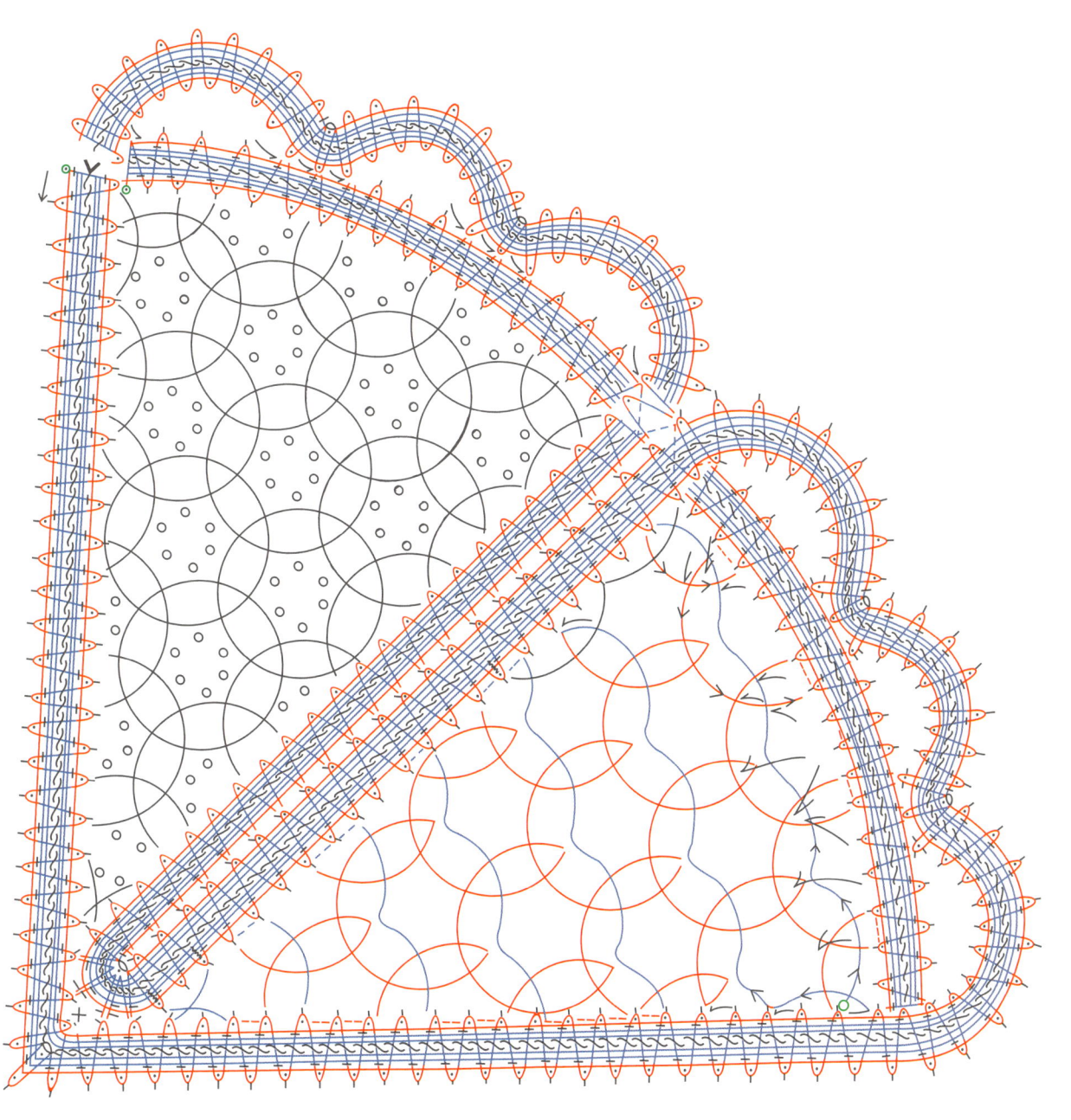

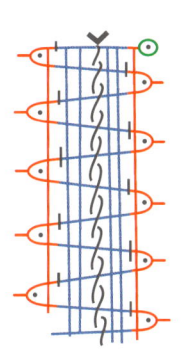

Diagram for Cone No. 10

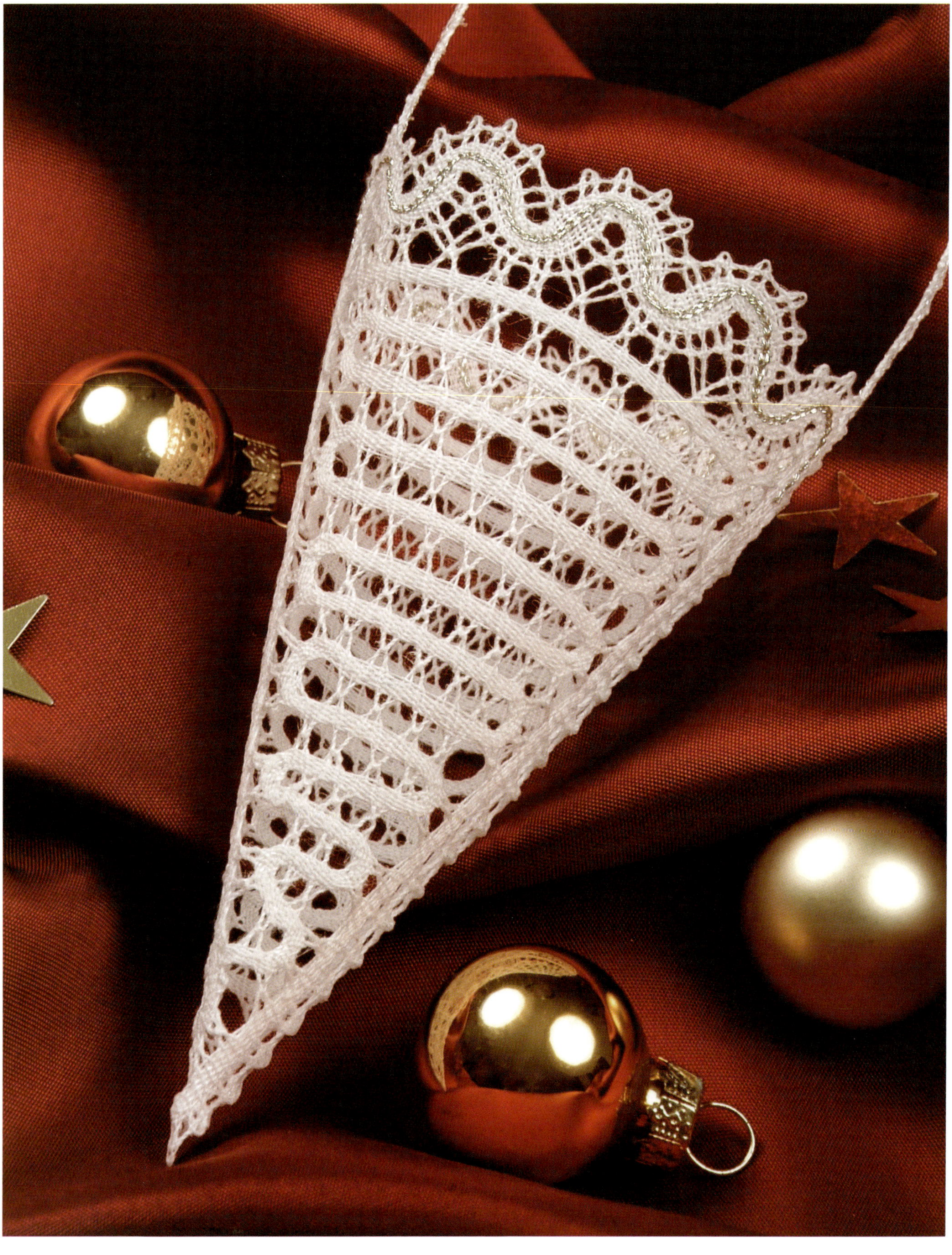

Cone No. 11 – Idrija Lace

Materials
7 pairs of linen 50/2
1 pair of DMC metallic thread, silver art. 283

The silver pairs are worked as chain stitches.
The twists and sew in marks apply for the entire piece.
Start the tape as indicated on the diagram, then add in the silver 2 pairs. At O add the 7th (and final) linen pair. Follow the diagram for the curved tape.
At the black marking ⚹ you must sew in, and the pair sewn in now works along the outher edge on the next curve. The same pair reverts to being the worker on the 3rd curve. Continue until you reach the straight tapes. Here you leave out one linen pair and the 2 silver pairs.
Now continue with 6 linen pairs for the straight tapes. Bring the pairs in again for the next half of the cone. The pairs are sewn into the starting loops and tied off.
For the filling, work the narrow whole stitch tapes with 5 linen pairs. Start at O on the right side.

The Handle
7 pairs of linen 60/2
1 pair of DMC metallic thread, silver art. 283
The full length of the handle is 20 cm.

The gold or silver thread is worked as chain stitch.

To Finish
The lace is starched heavily.
Stitch the cone together loop to loop with a thinner thread e.g. linen 80/2.
Stitch on the handle.

Pricking for Cone No. 11

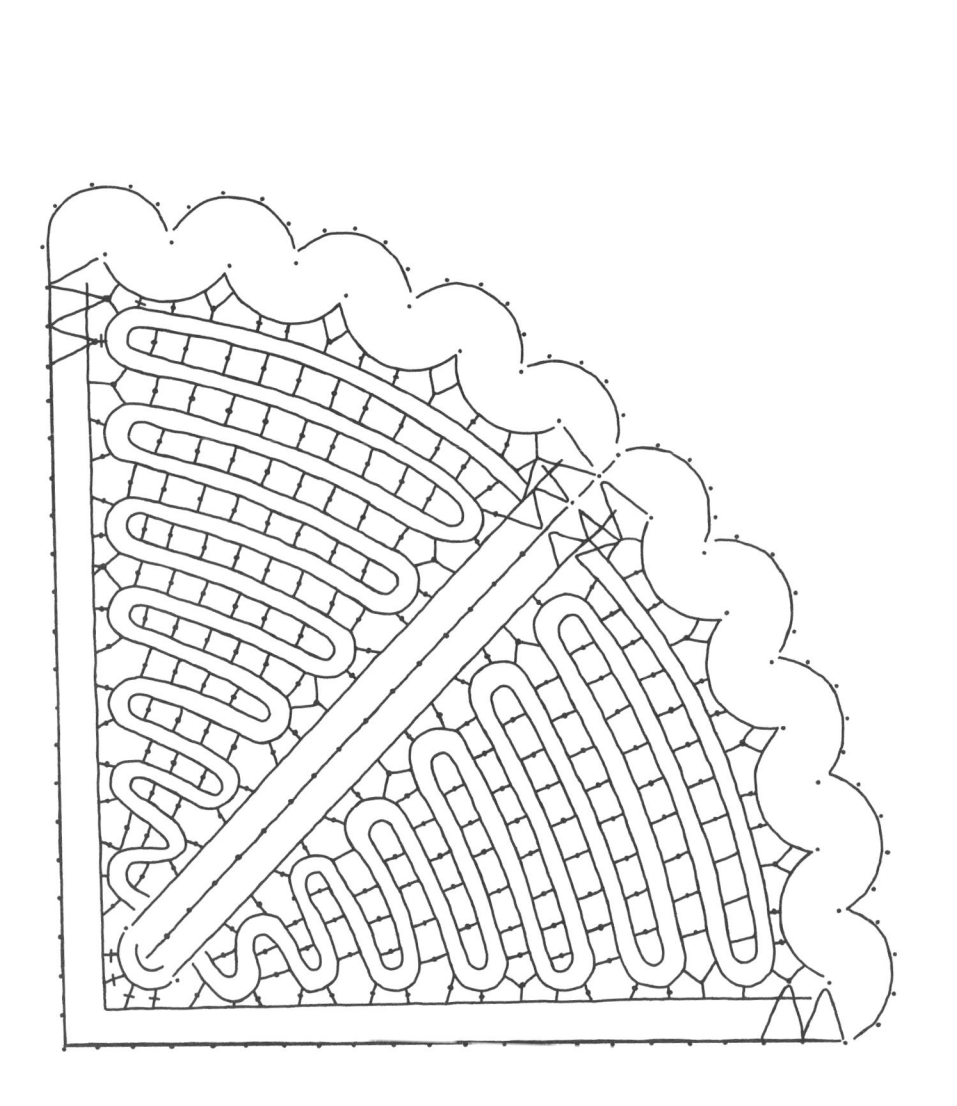

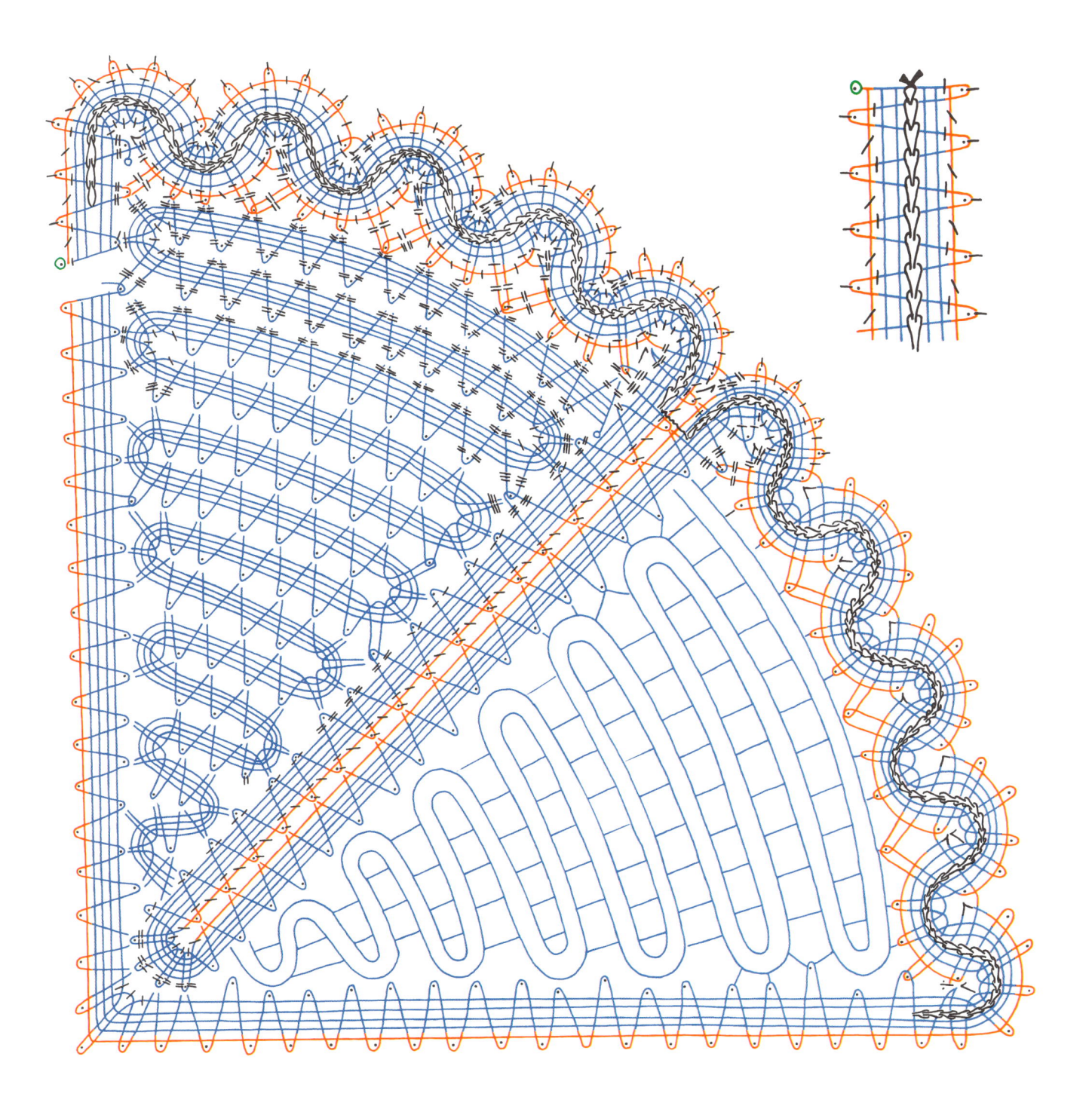

Diagram for Cone No. 11

63

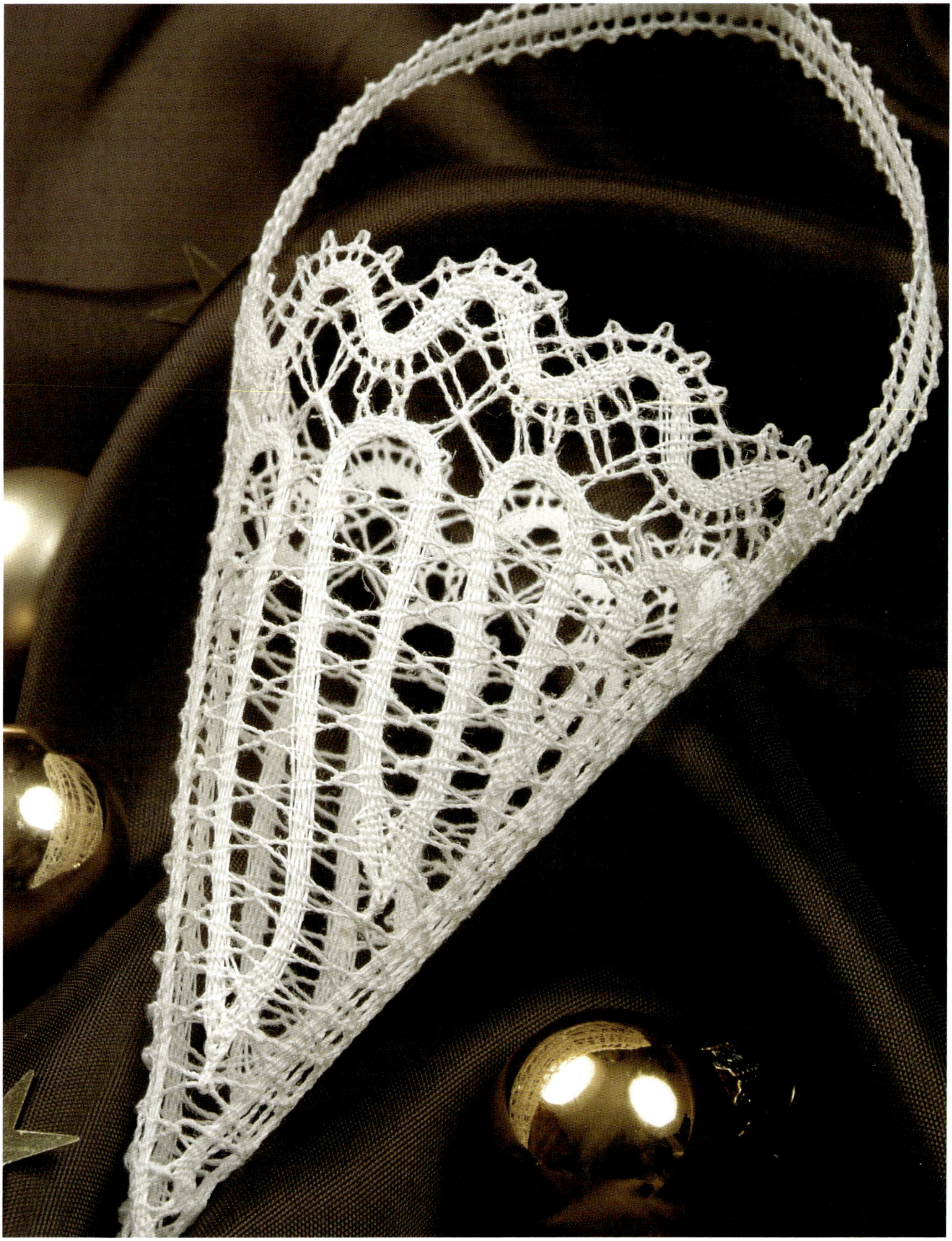

Cone No. 12 – Idrija Lace

Materials
7 pairs of linen 50/2

The twists and sew in marks apply for the entire piece.
Start the tape as indicated on the diagram. At ◯ add the 7th (and final) pair. Follow the diagram for the curved tape.
At the black marking ⚹ you must sew in. The pair sewn in works along the outer edge on the next curve. The same pair reverts to being the worker on the 3rd curve. Continue until you reach the straight tapes. Here you leave out one pair and the straight tapes are worked with 6 pairs.
Bring the pair back in for the next half of the cone. Continue all the way round. The pairs are sewn into the starting loops and are tied off.
To finish, work the narrow whole stitch tapes with 5 linen pairs. You will find the technical drawings for the narrow tapes on page 19.

The Handle
7 pairs of linen 60/2
The full length of the handle is 19 cm.

The Finish
The lace is starched heavily.
Stitch the cone together loop to loop with a thinner thread e.g. linen 80/2.
Stitch on the handle.

Pricking for Cone No. 12

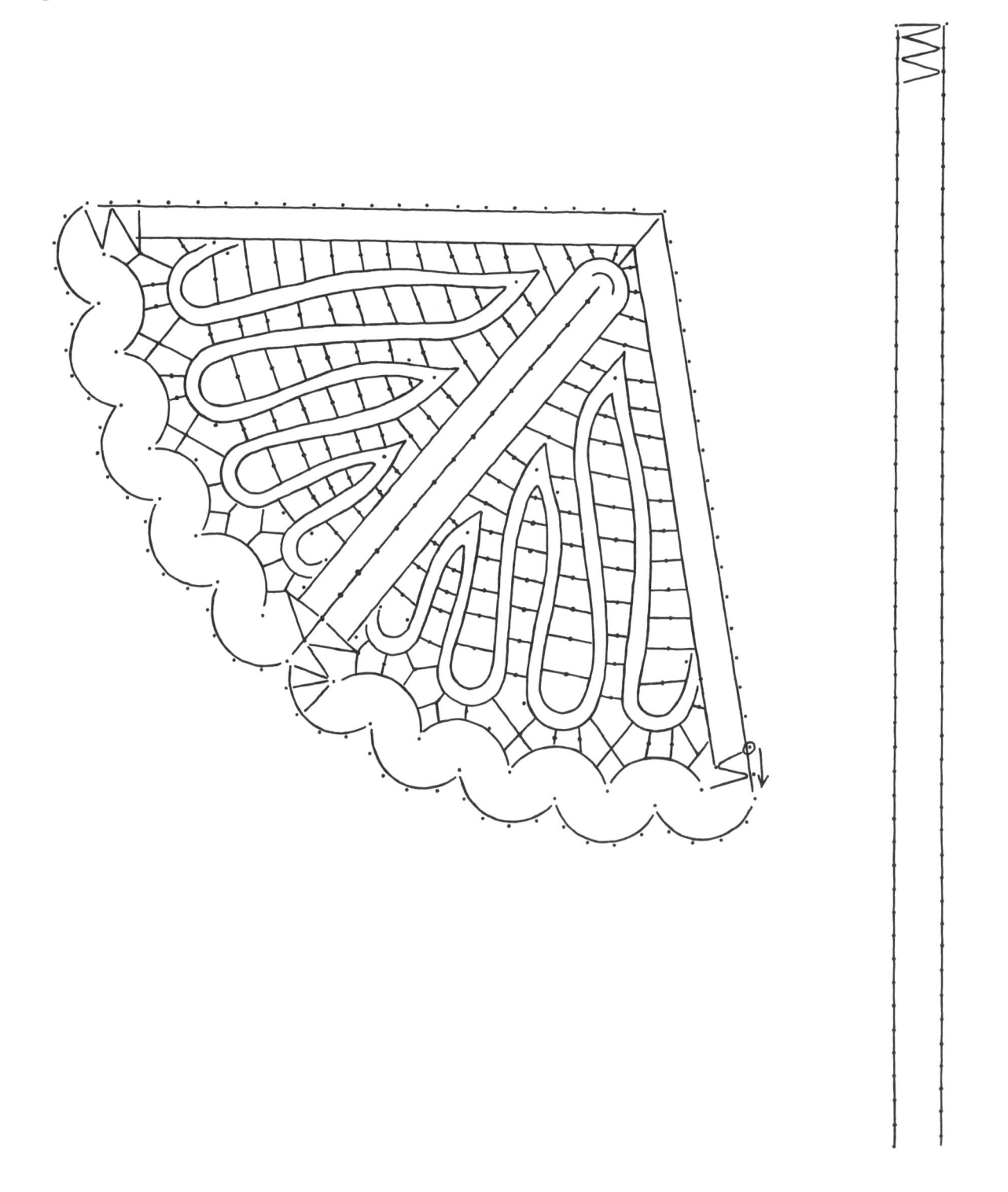

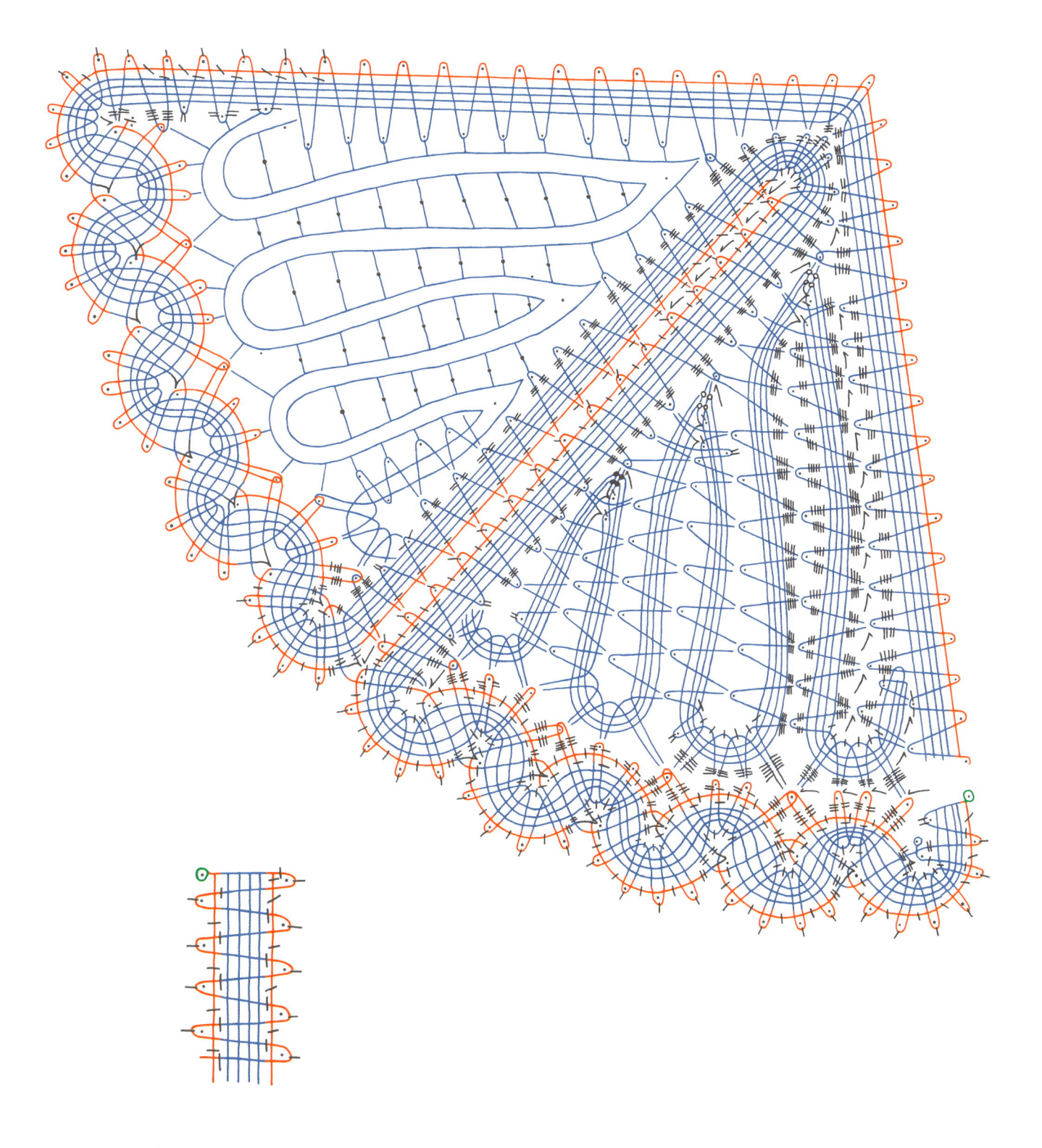

Diagram for Cone No. 12

67

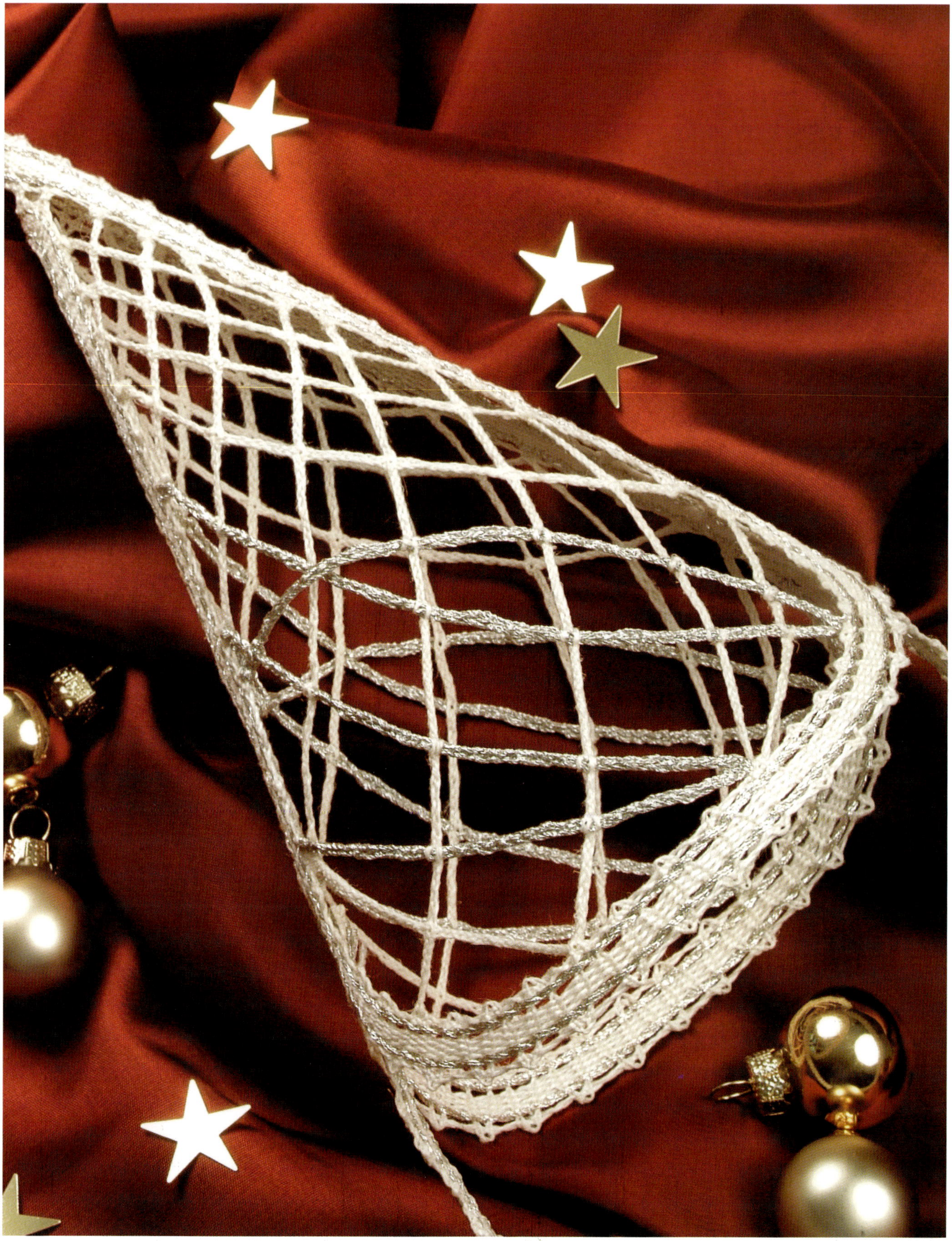

Cone No. 13 – Free Style Filling

Materials
6 pairs of linen 16/2
2 pairs DMC Mouliné, silver art. 317 (2 bunches of thread)

Use 5 threads from the silver Mouliné. Take the full length and divide into pairs – then there ought to be enough thread to last for the filling which is worked with the silver thread. The 2 silver pairs are used in the tape as contour stitches.
Start the tape at the mark and follow the diagram all the way round. Remember the extra twists at the pin holes where you are going to sew in later. Sew in at the starting loops.
If you have plenty of thread on the worker pair and the outer pair – use them for the filling. Reuse as many of the pairs from the tape as possible – also the silver pairs – because then these pairs are secured at the same time. The other pairs are finished off with a row of knots.

The Filling
The filling is plaited.
10 pairs of linen 16/2
2 pairs of DMC Mouliné, silver art. 317

Start working the plaits with the silver thread (marked in blue) and finish them. The heavy silver thread is tied off with a small roll of 3-4 half hitches, p. 17.
Then sew in the linen pairs when you need them. When a plait crosses a silver plait, sew in with the technique from p. 12 (2 plaits crossing).
At all other points, 2 plaits cross in a windmill crossing, p. 11.
When necessary, the plait sews in and changes direction. Where it ends, make a small roll of 3-4 half hitches.
Dotted line, the plait runs along the edge – sew in if necessary – see diagram p. 71.

The Handle
6 pairs of linen 16/2
2 pairs of DMC Mouliné, silver art. 317
The full length of the handle is 41 cm.

The silver thread is worked as a contour thread.

To Finish
The lace is starched heavily.
Stitch the cone together loop to loop, start from the bottom. End with a false plait = a bar where you make bottom hole stitches around. The stitching together is done with a thinner thread e.g. linen 40/2. Stitch on the handle.

Pricking for Cone No. 13

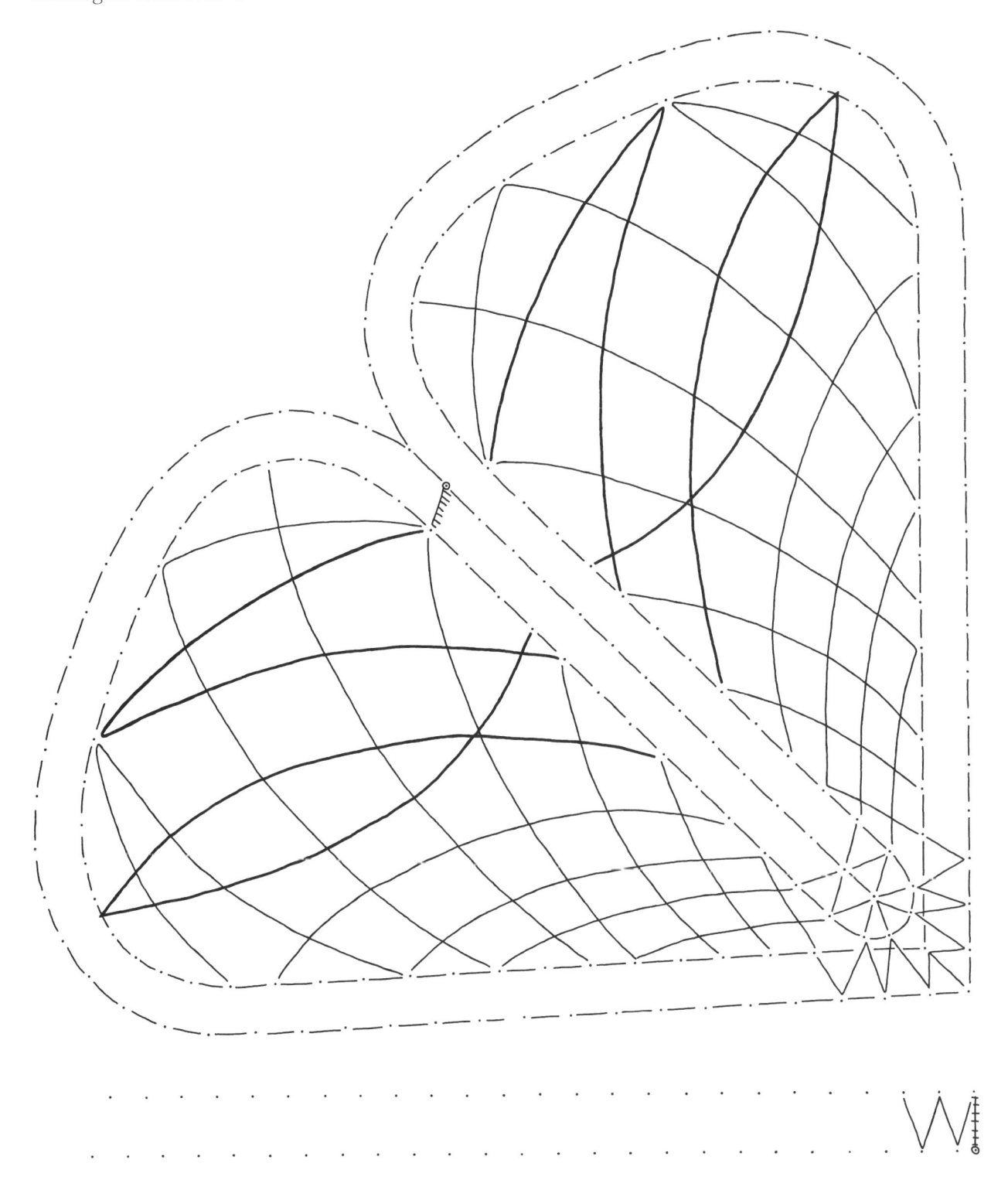

Set the copier at 125 %

Diagram for Cone No. 13

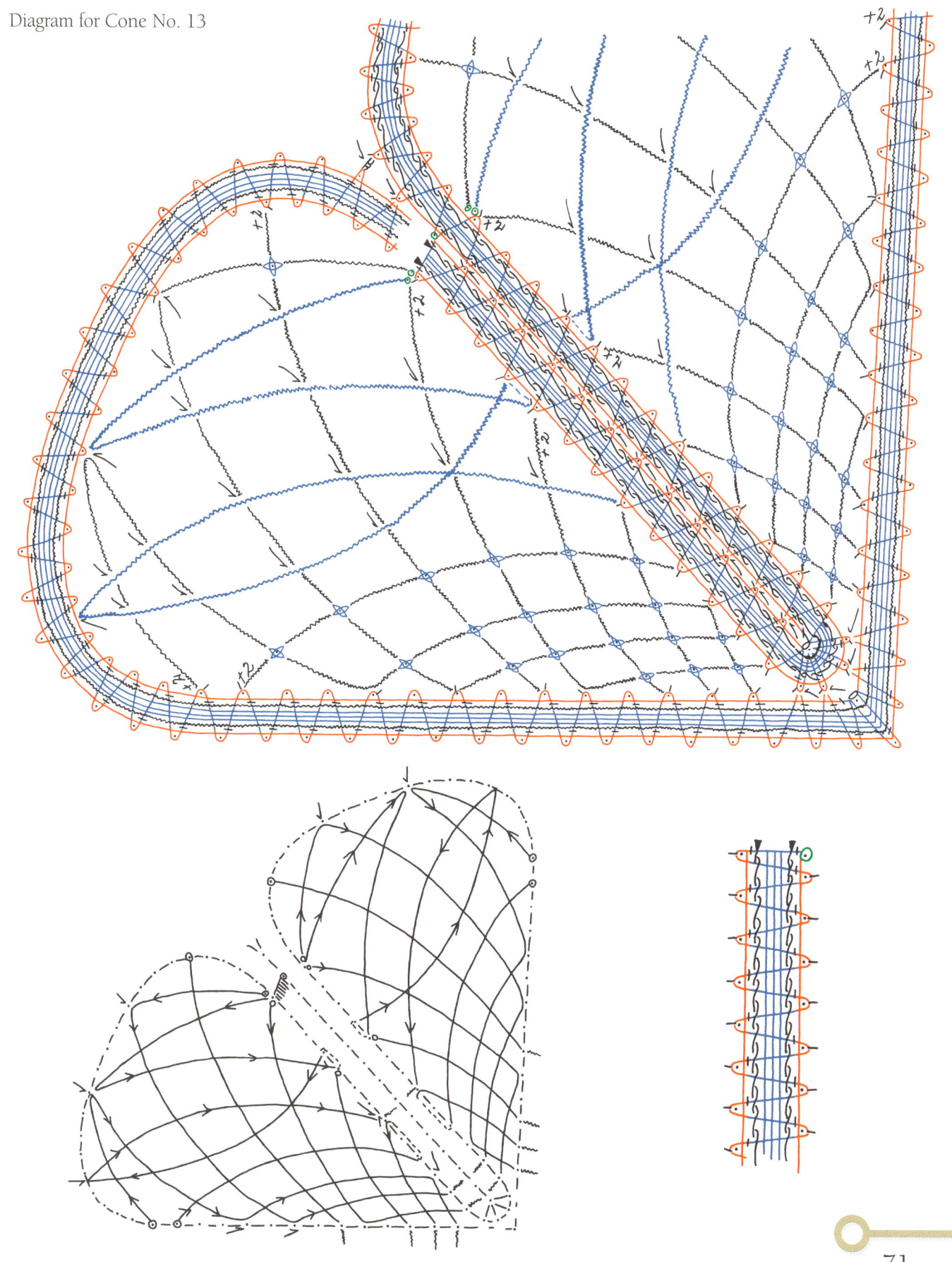

71

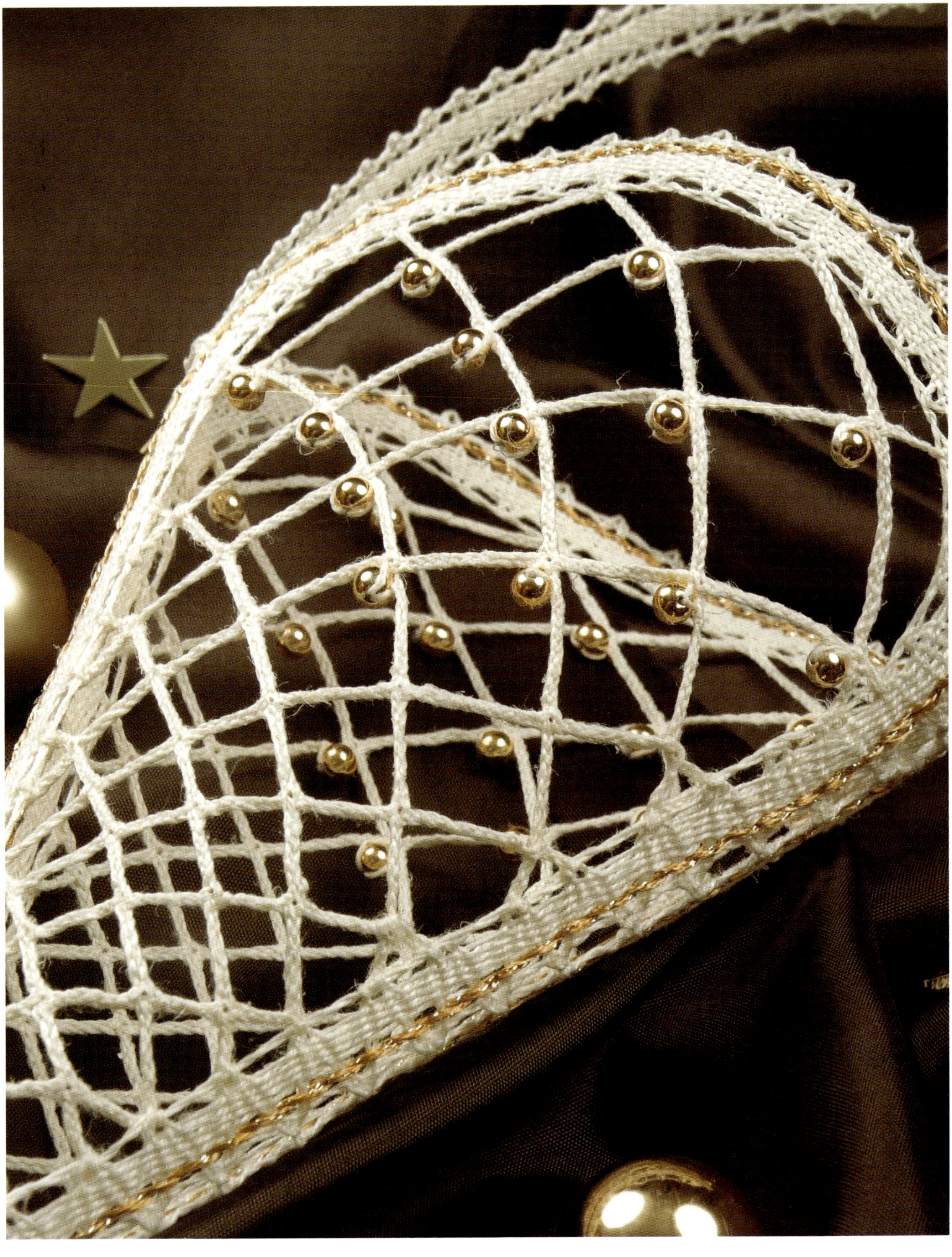

Cone No. 14
– with plaits and beads

Materials
7 pairs of linen 16/2
1 pair of DMC Mouliné, gold art. 317 (1 bunch of thread)
26 pearls, gold 5 mm

Use 5 threads from the gold Mouliné.
One pair of gold is worked as contour stitches in the tape.
Start the tape at the mark and follow the diagram all the way round. Sew in at the starting loops and tie off by making a small roll with 3-4 half hitches, p. 17.
If you have got plenty of thread on the worker and the inner edge pairs, use them for the filling. Reuse 2 more pairs from the tape if possible. Then make a small plait to get the pairs ready for the pinhole where the pairs are sewn in.

The Filling
12 pairs of linen 16/2 + the beads

The filling is plaits with beads.
When 2 plaits cross, work a windmill crossing p. 11. Add the pearl – see p. 18 and then continue with the plaits.
At the dotted line the plait runs along the edge – sew in if necessary – see diagram p. 75.

The Handle
7 pairs of linen 16/2
The full length of the handle is 41 cm.

The Finish
The lace is starched heavily.
Stitch the cone together loop to loop with a thinner thread e.g. linen 40/2.
Finish by making the last false plait with needle and thread.
Stitch on the handle.

Pricking for Cone No. 14

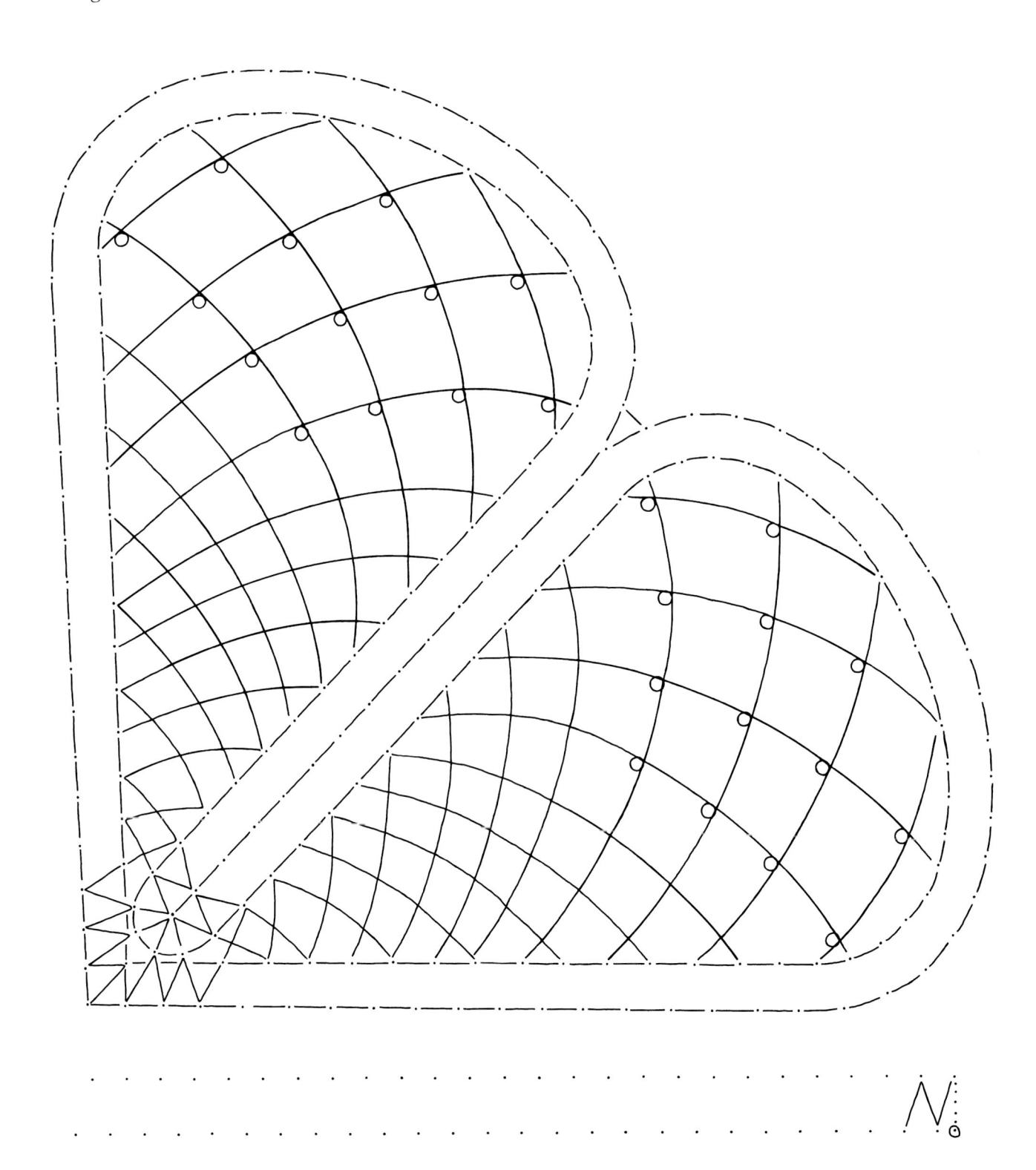

Set the copier at 125 %

Diagram for Cone No. 14

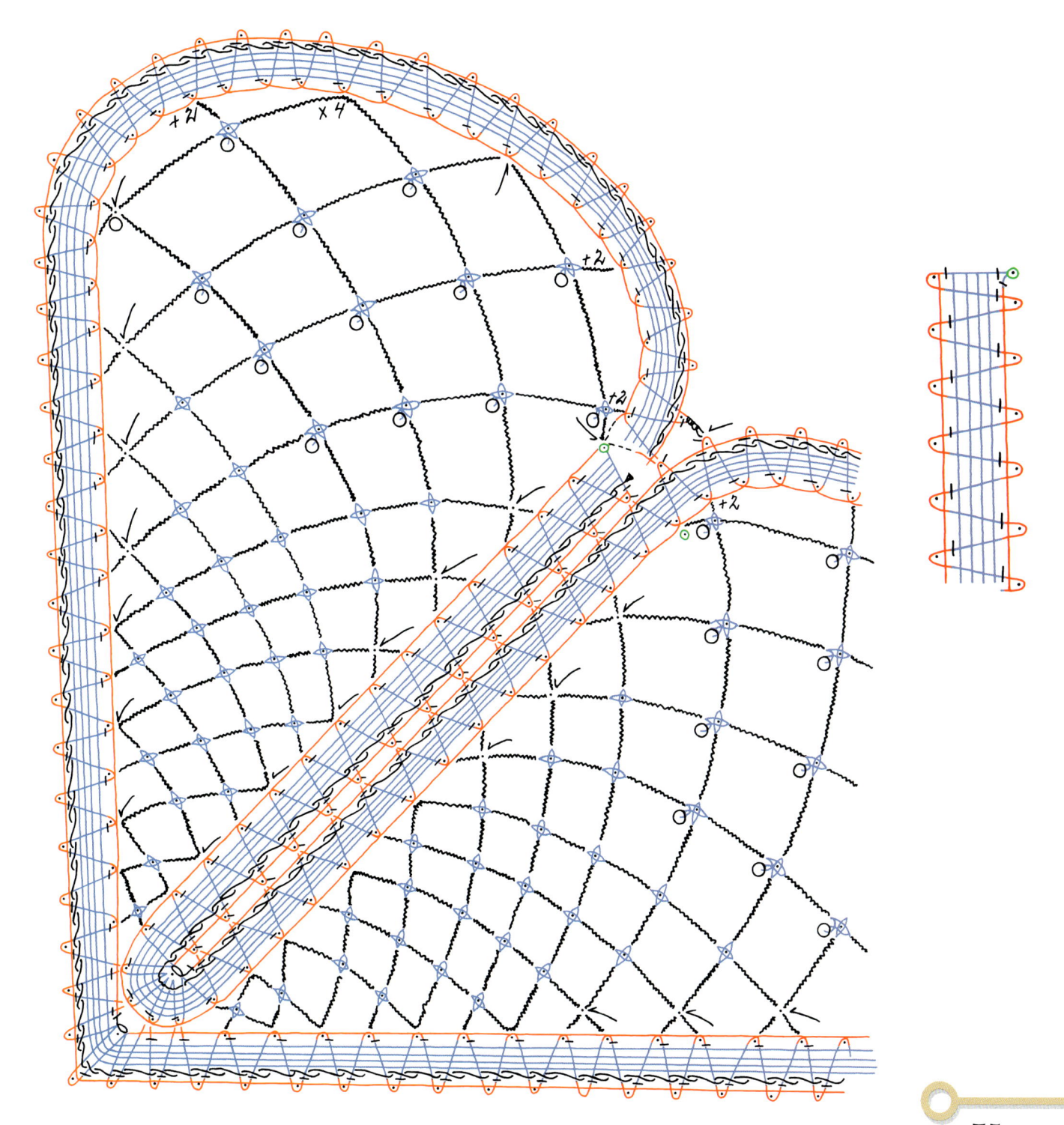

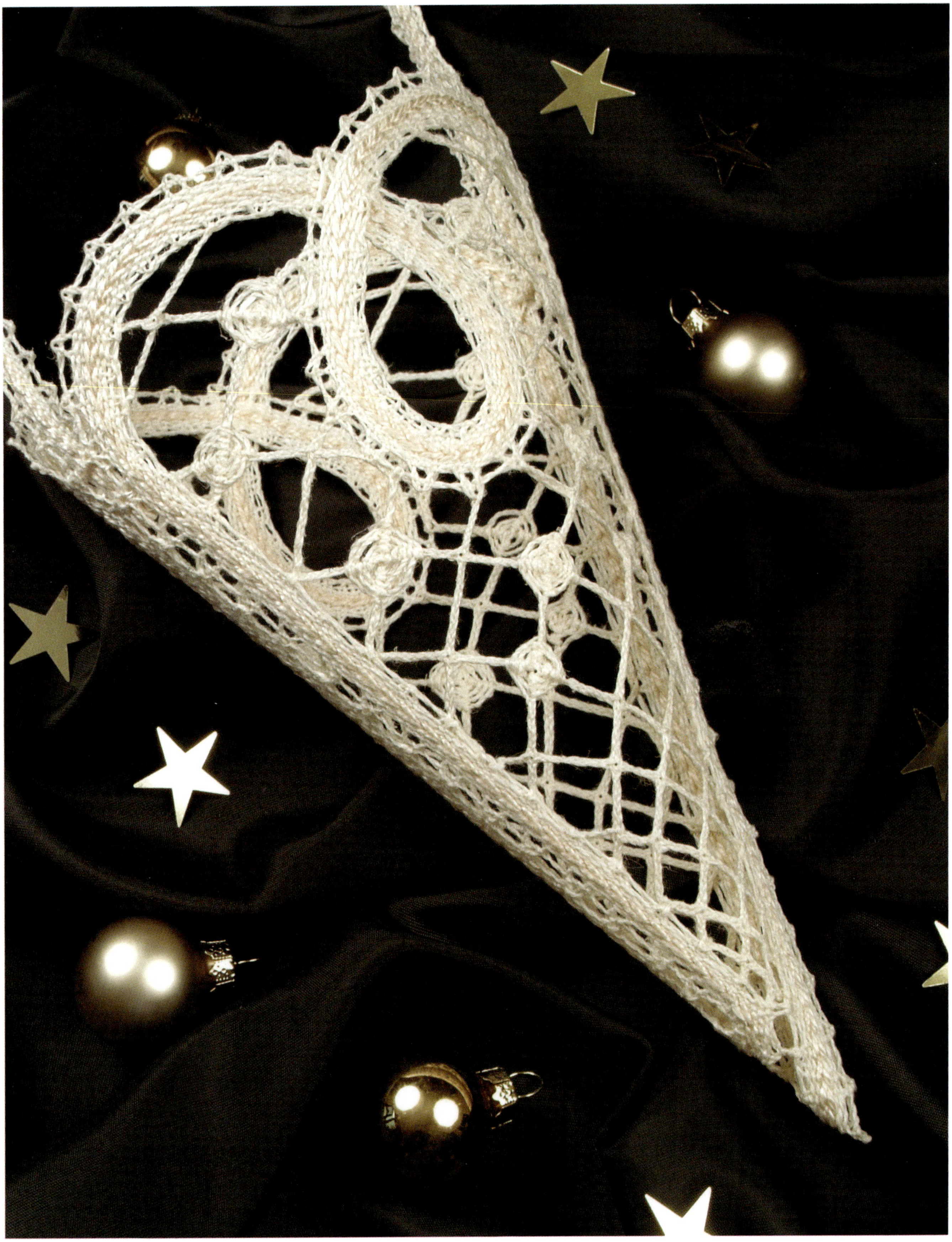

Cone No. 15
– with Russian spiders

Materials
7 pairs of linen 16/2
2 pairs of DMC pearl nr. 3 Ecu – or similar

The 2 pairs of pearl are worked in the tape as chain stitches.
Start the tape at the mark and follow the diagram all the way round. The small diagram shows how the tape crosses the tape. Sew into the starting loops and tie off with a row of knots.

The Filling
12 pairs of linen 16/2

The filling is plaits and Russian spiders, see p. 16.
Follow the small diagram.
The plaits cross with a windmill crossing, p. 11. Where 2 plaits are sewn together, work method 2, p. 14.
All the plaits ends with a roll of half hitches, p. 17.

The Handle
7 pairs of linen 16/2
2 pairs of DMC pearl nr. 3
The full length of the handle is 41 cm.

To Finish
The lace is starched heavily.
Stitch the cone together loop to loop with a thinner thread e.g. linen 40/2.
Finish by making the last false plait with needle and thread.
Stitch on the handle.

Pricking for Cone No. 15

Set the copier at 150 %

Diagram for Cone No. 15

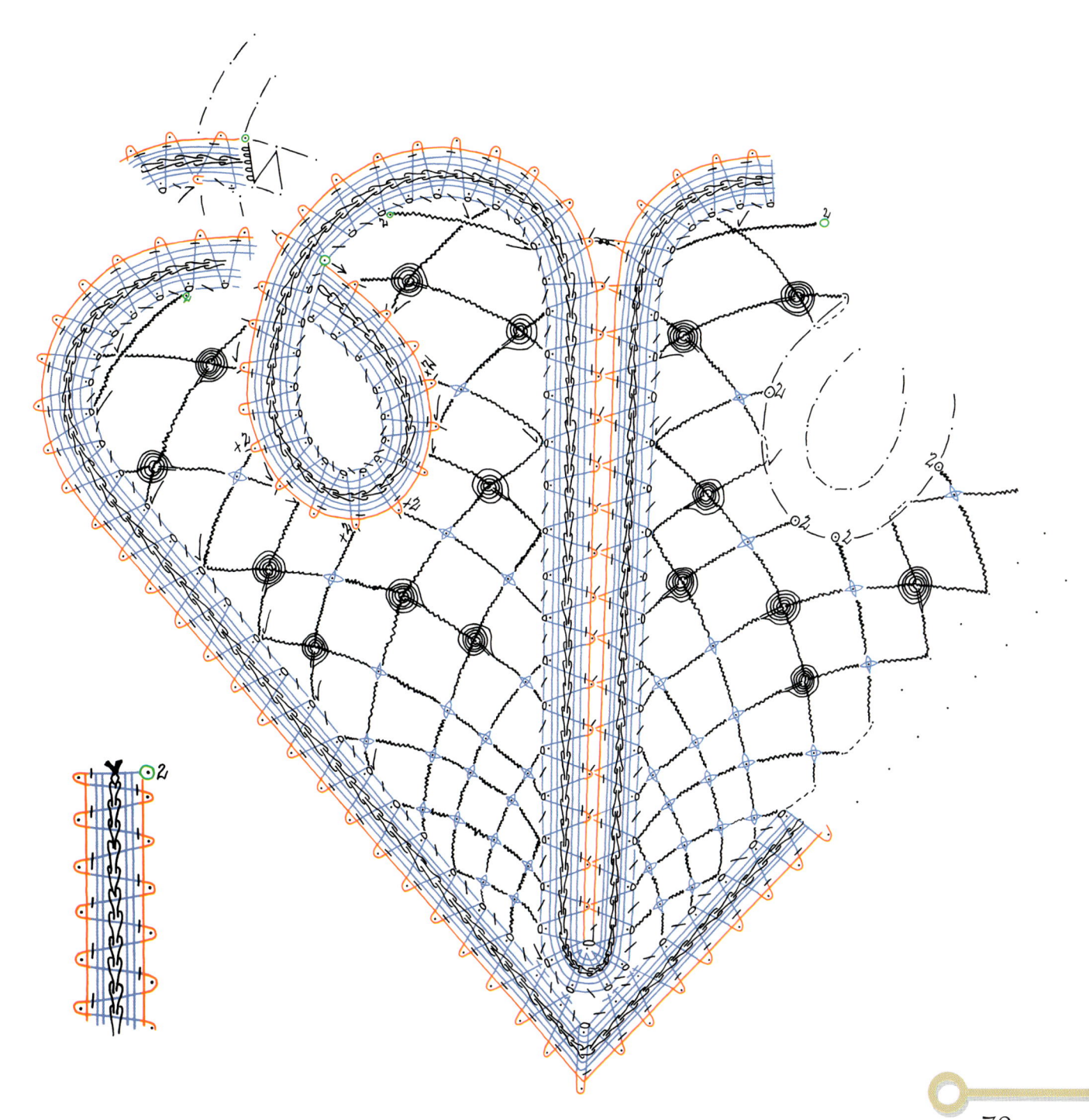

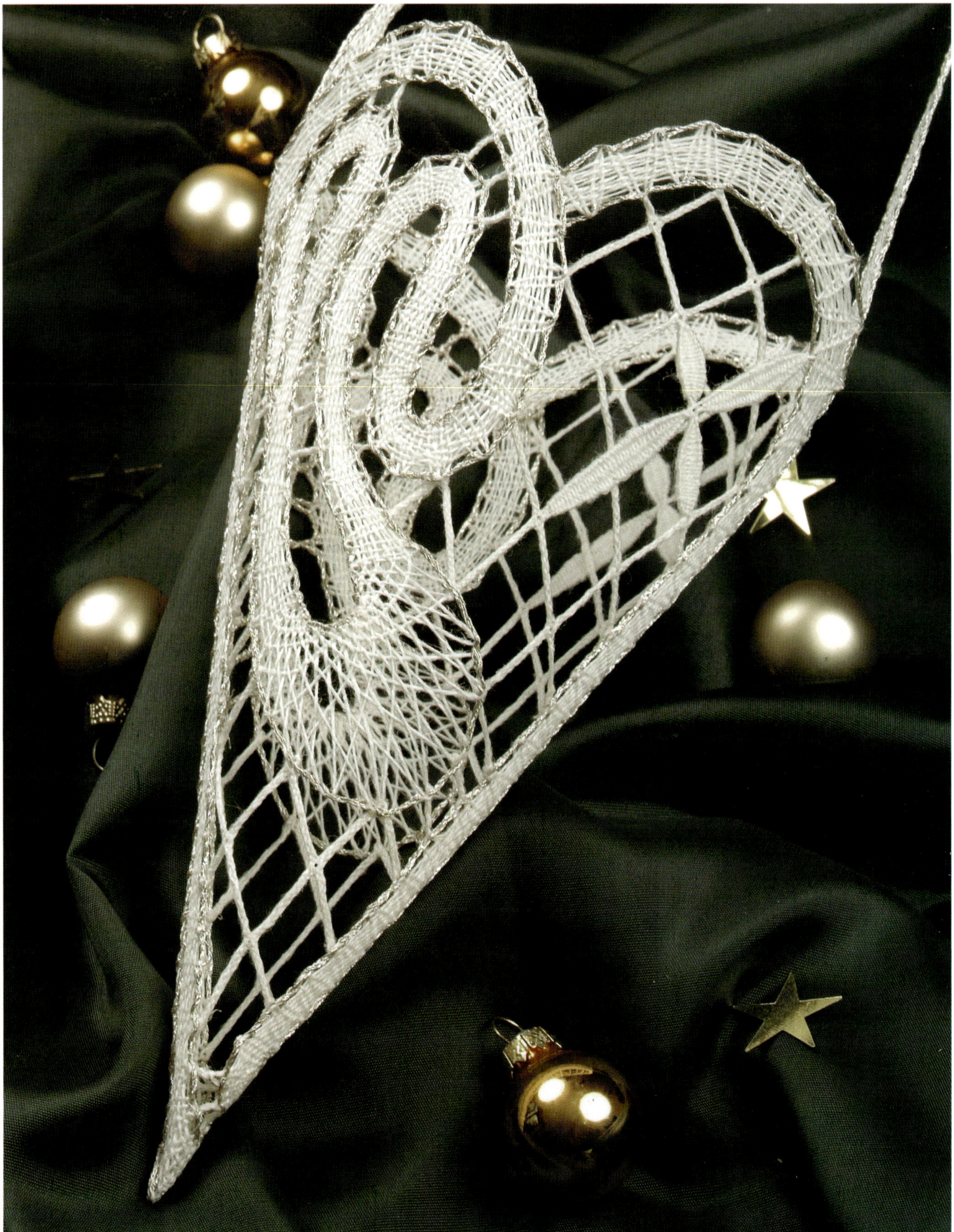

Cone No. 16
– with an asymmetric tape

Materials
5 pairs of linen 20/2 or 30/3
2 pairs of DMC Mouliné, silver art. 317 (1 bunch of thread)

The twists and sew in marks apply for the entire piece.
Use 3 silver threads for each pair and work the silver pairs in the tape as contour stitches.
Start the outher tape on the left side with 2 silver pairs and the workers. Then add the last 4 pairs, see diagram 1 on p. 83. The tape is worked in whole stitch with turn stitch at both sides. Where indicated the workers go through the silver pair and the 2 tapes are joined with false plaits, see diagram 2. The sewing in is done as shown on p. 9.
Complete the first tape.
The next tape begins at 2. Start the pairs just behind tape 1 – the small black dots. Continue all the way round. At the end the pairs again overlap tape 1 a little. Place a pin between each pair and tie off with a row of knots up towards the pins. If there's enough thread on the bobbins, use the workers and the inner pair for the plait.

The Filling
10 pairs of linen 20/2 or 30/3

The filling is plaited.
All the plaits cross with a windmill crossing – see p. 11
All plaits are tied off with 4-5 half hitches, p. 17.
The leaves are worked first because the right side of the work is facing the pillow. The plait is worked on top of the leaves = the dotted line – see diagram 3.

The Handle
5 pairs of linen 20/2 or 30/3
2 pairs of DMC silver
The full length of the handle is 38 cm.

The Finish
The lace is starched heavily.
Stitch the cone together loop to loop with a thinner thread e.g. linen 40/2.
Finish by making the last false plait with needle and thread.
Stitch on the handle.

Pricking for Cone No. 16

Set the copier at 125 %

diagram 3

Diagram for Cone No. 16

○ Linen thread
● Gold- or silver thread

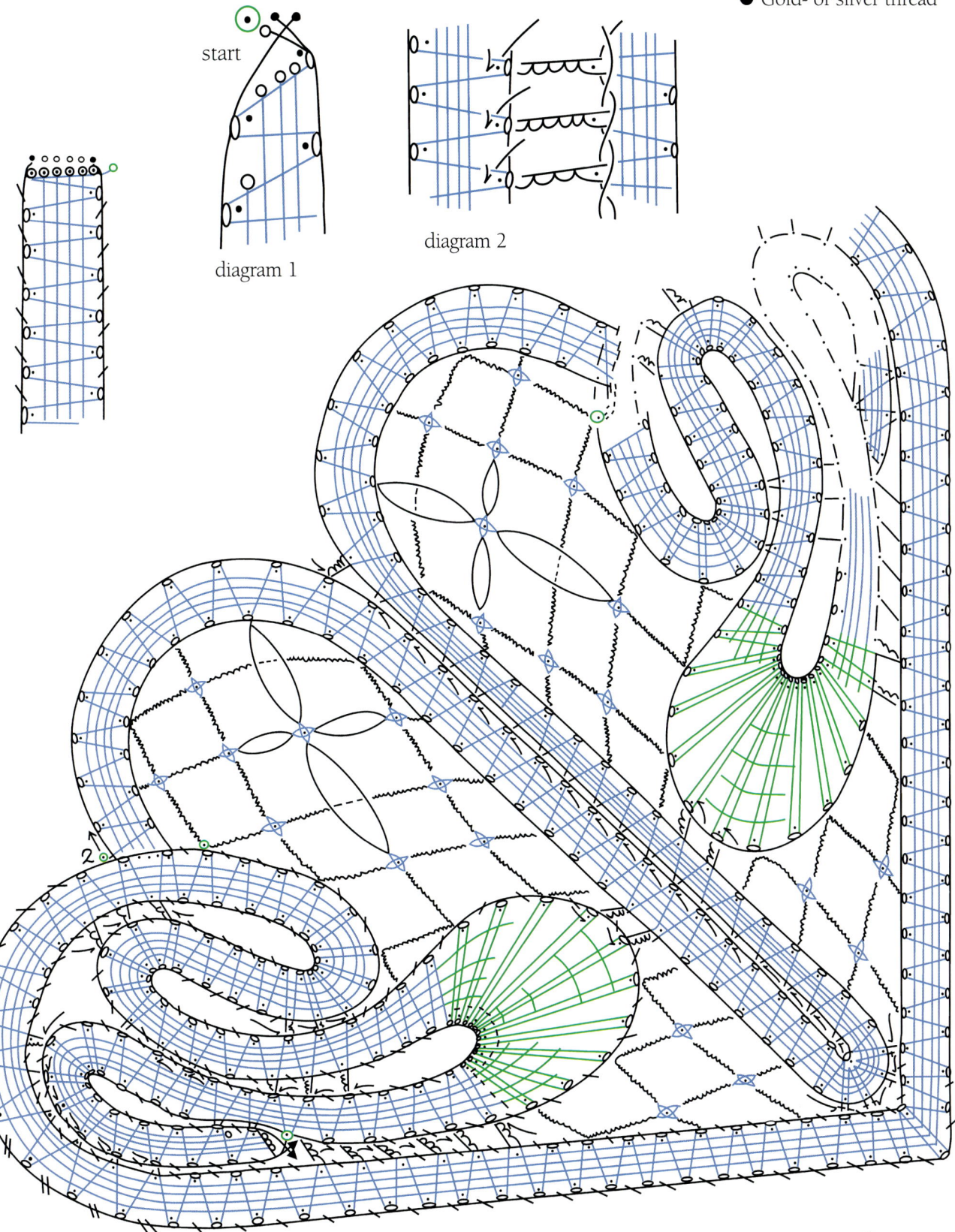

start

diagram 1

diagram 2

83

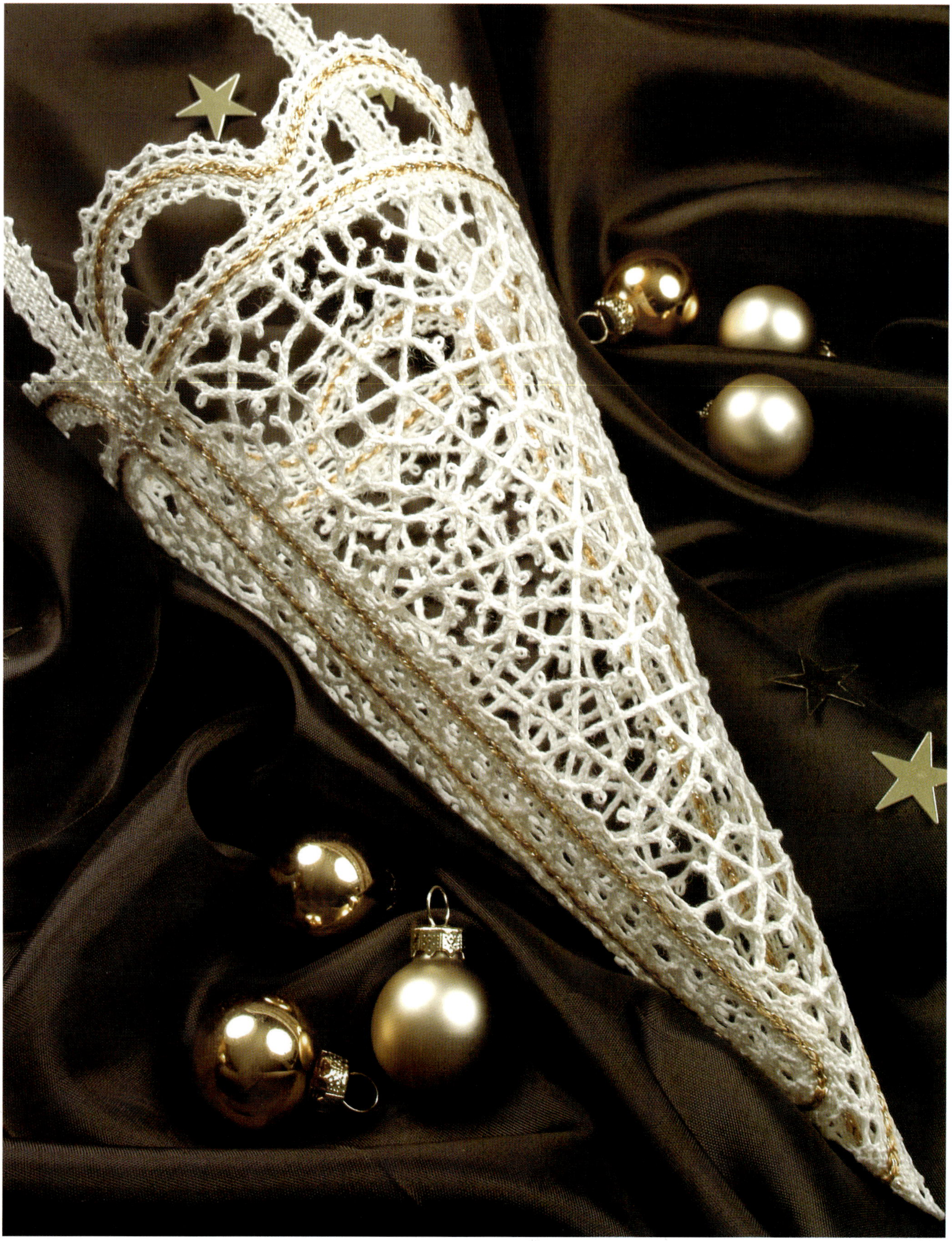

Cone No. 17 – Russian Tape Lace

Materials
7 pairs of linen 16/2
2 pairs of DMC Mouliné, gold art. 317 (1 bunch of thread)

The twists and sew in marks apply for the entire piece.
Use 4 gold threads for each pair and work the gold pairs in the tape as chain stitches.
Start the tape at the mark and continue all the way round. Sew in at the starting loops and tie off in a row of knots. If there is enough thread on the bobbins reuse them for the horizontal tapes. Continue working over the vertical tapes, following the dotted line.

The Filling
The filling is worked in plaits and picots – 2 thread picots with only 4 twists in this coarse thread – p. 15.
First follow the red line all the way round and continue into the blue line. This is followed until the line stops at the horizontal tape. Start again with the green line in the middle of the horizontal tape and follow this until it ends on the opposite vertical tape. To finish, follow the short green line across the point of the cone.
Some places there are many plaits to be joined; use either method 1 or method 2 on p. 13 or p. 14. Remember, no sewing in until the last time you pass the point where a join is needed.
Tie off the plaits with a small roll of half hitches, p. 17.

The Handle
8 pairs of linen 16/2
The full length of the handle is 46 cm.

The Finish
The lace is starched heavily.
Stitch the cone together loop to loop with a thinner thread e.g. linen 40/2.
Stitch on the handle.

Pricking for Cone No. 17

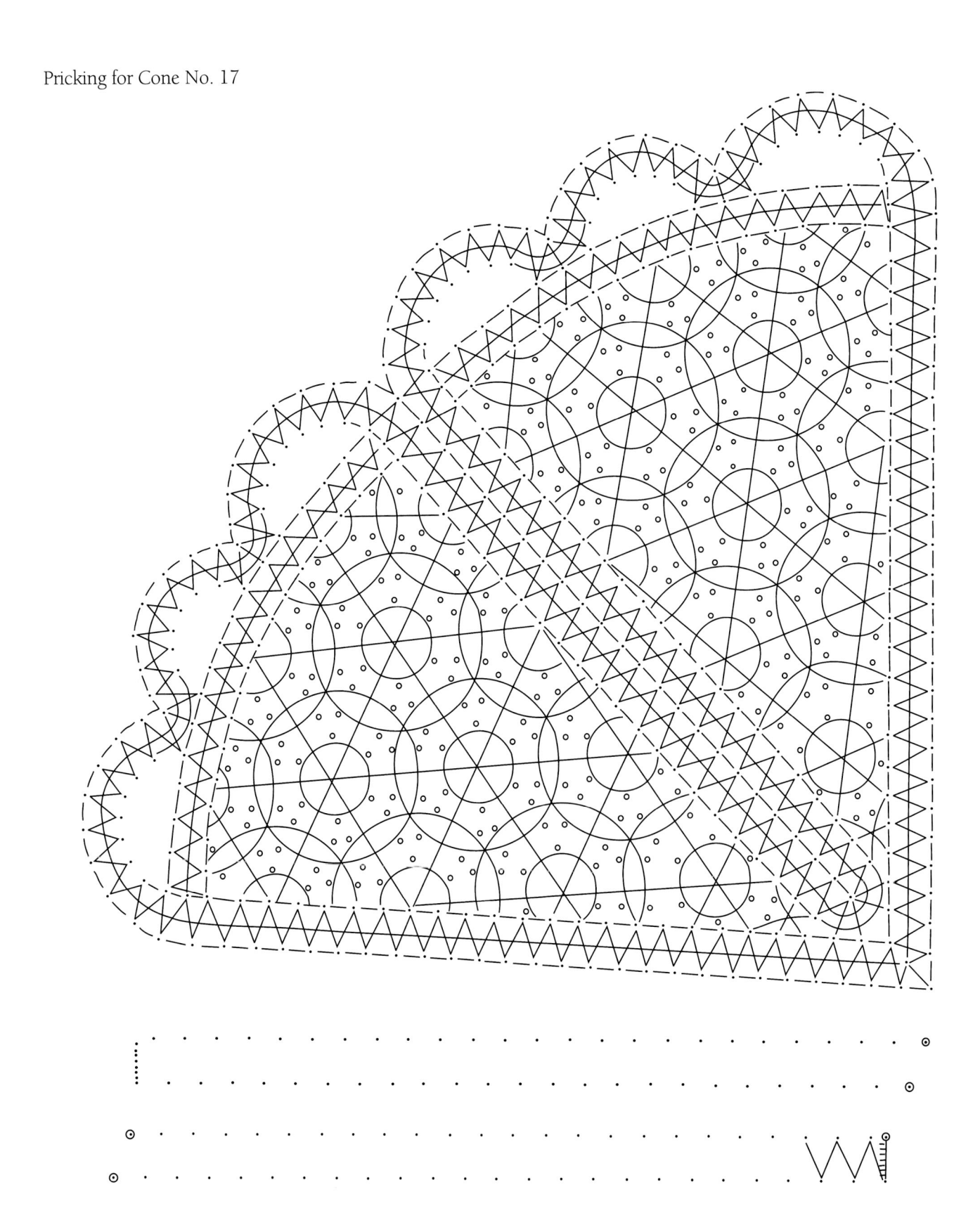

Set the copier at 150 %

Diagram for Cone No. 17

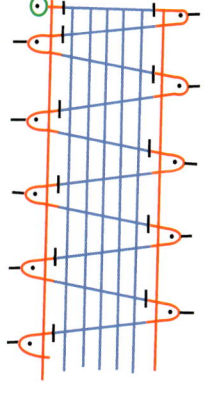

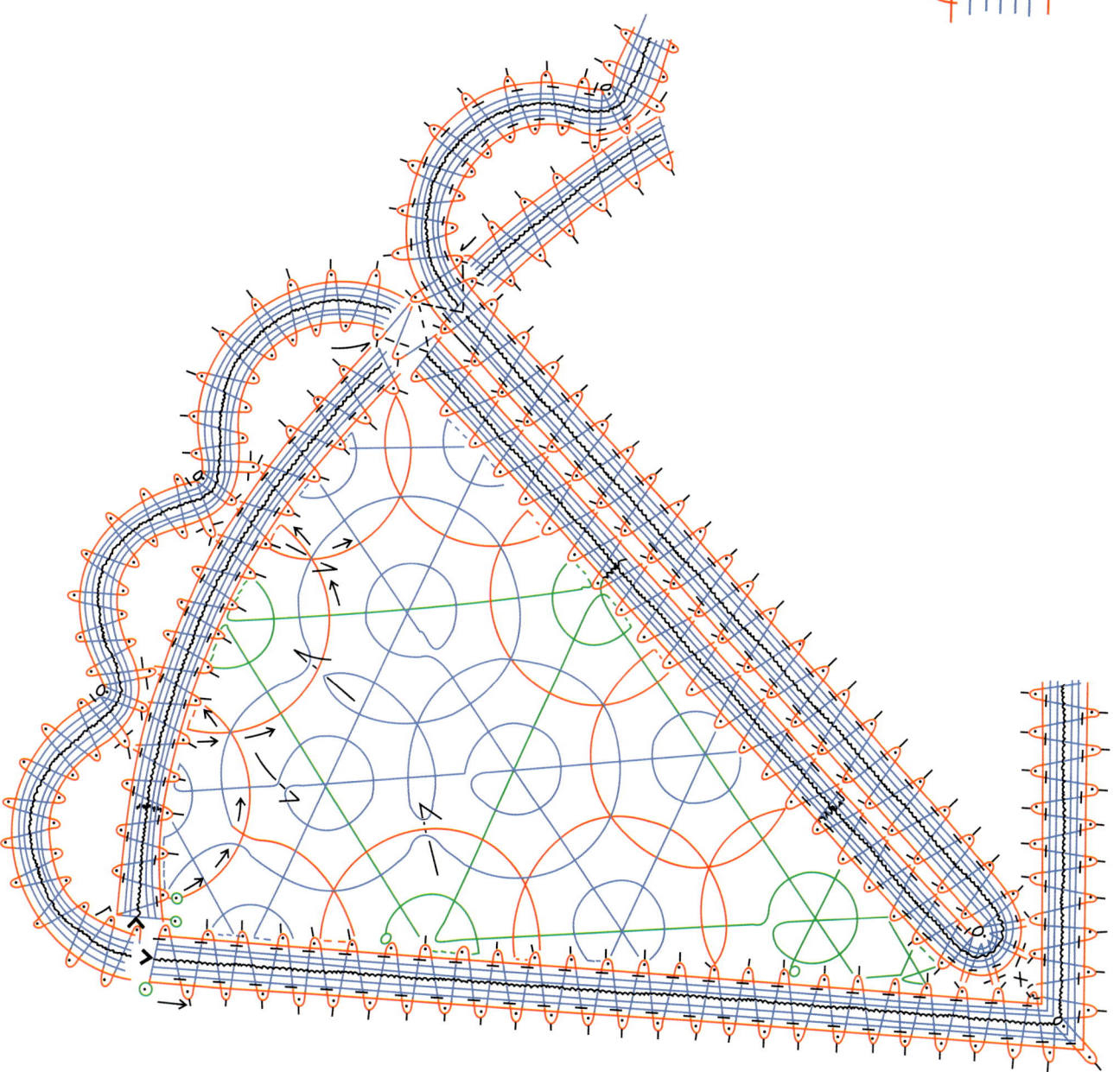